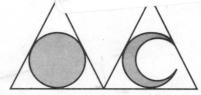

Council of Light, Inc.
presents

*A*SCENSION
The
Time
Has
Come . . .

**An Enlightening View From Masters
Who Have Ascended**

**By Renowned Spiritual Teacher,
Shaman, and Channel for the Masters**

Bob Fickes

First edition published in 1991 by:
Council of Light, Inc.
P. O. Box 670
Mount Shasta, California 96067-9998

Assisting Mr. Fickes in transcription,
editing, and formatting: Candace Welter

Photo: James Scott

©Cover Art and Design: Sherri Vicars

Registered in the United States
Printed in Chiang Mai, Thailand

I S B N 1-56601-000-4

A Warm and Special Thanks:
to the most beautiful spirit in my life, my wife, Linda,
for her gracious love, comfort, and support,
to the special joy in my life, my daughter, Alana, for all
the light and happiness she has brought me,
and to Candace, for her assistance in formulating
these powerful teachings for publication.

TABLE OF
CONTENTS

ABOUT THE AUTHOR AND FOUNDER OF THE COUNCIL OF LIGHT, INC.

BOB FICKES:

Bob Fickes is an extraordinary spiritual teacher to thousands throughout the world, with nearly twenty-five (25) years experience and a Masters Degree in the Science of Creative Intelligence from Maharishi European Research University in Switzerland. He is an exceptionally clear, and fully conscious representative (channel) for the Ascended Masters. Under their loving direction, Bob founded The Council of Light, Inc. in 1986.

As a young boy, Bob discovered new dimensions of communication beyond the physical, including the realms of Archangels and Ascended Masters. His extensive research in the field of Consciousness and Meditation, more than 80,000 hours spent in deep meditation, and numerous experiences under the guidance of the Indian Master Maharishi Mahesh Yogi, have served to deepen this gift, and advance Bob's understanding. He feels deeply fortunate to have enjoyed many private discussions with the Maharishi concerning his experiences. Over time, Bob has enhanced his extraordinary gifts and developed techniques to insure clear channeling from one's Higher Self, also called the Inner Christ Consciousness. For many years, Bob kept his experiences private, sharing them only with the Maharishi, and his close friends and relatives. It was not until early adulthood that Bob began to share his gifts with others—going public as a Conscious Channel (that is, one who does not go into a trance).

As one of the first Teachers and Coordinators of the Transcendental Meditation Movement in the United States in the late 1960's and early 1970's, Bob was instrumental in pioneering its acceptance within communities, universities, hospitals, prisons, and drug rehabilitation programs throughout the Eastern United States. His design of curriculum for the Science of Creative Intelligence was among the first to be offered and accepted into the Philadelphia Secondary Public School System and George School of Bucks County, Pennsylvania. Among his many other accomplishments, Bob is proud to have been one of the first Teachers to bring Transcendental Meditation to the Federal Penitentiary of Warwick Rhode Island, the Pennsylvania State Hospital for Mental Health in Harrisburg, Pennsylvania, where the need was truly great, and also to the Institute for Living in Hartford, Connecticut.

From 1977 to 1981, Bob was instrumental in establishing the first New Age Television Station in the world, KSCI channel 18 in Los Angeles. Broadcasting 3.3 million watts of power on UHF, their signal spanned from Santa Barbara to San Diego. KSCI offered programming for the Age of Enlightenment such as positive news and world trends, health for enlightenment, meditation programs, and other related information. He served as Program Director of KSCI in his last years at the station.

Over the years, Bob has travelled throughout the United States, Canada, and Europe sharing Consciousness and Enlightenment with thousands in New York, Los Angeles, Berkeley, and Washington, D.C., including movie and recording stars, and several well known financial consultants. Bob now travels throughout Asia teaching his techniques and insights. His work is featured around the world in a variety of magazines, newsletters, and local publications, and in over forty channeled audio cassettes distributed throughout the world. He does private sessions both in person and by telephone to over 3,500 clients all over the globe, and has published over fifty different articles in *The Connecting Link, Challenge Magazine, Spirit Speaks,* and other similar publications, and additional books that will expand on Ascension, Enlightenment, Holistic Healing and the role of the Healer are in preparation for publication. As a recognized and highly respected Teacher of Meditation, and unusually clear Channel for the Ascended Masters and the Angelic Realm, Bob is highly respected and admired by his peers in the Spiritual and "New Age" community, and has appeared on several network television programs over the past few years, including the ABC Evening News in Honolulu.

Bob has now settled in Honolulu, Hawaii where he resides with his lovely, talented wife and partner, Dr. Linda Fickes, Chiropractor, and their daughter, Alana. Together they have established the Council of Light Inc. a center for Consciousness, Enlightenment and Healing in Honolulu.

THE COUNCIL OF LIGHT, INC.:

The Council of Light, Inc. integrates spiritual consciousness with the healing arts, including channeling and counseling services, chiropractic and massage therapies, chakra clearing and balancing, kundalini and god/goddess energy work, ancestral past life regression and clearing, and nutritional guidance and body work designated to accelerate and perfect the cellular crystalline matrix of the body.

This work creates an Accelerated Transformation Program™ for all dimensions of your existence. The Council of Light, Inc. is a vehicle for connecting you to the Ascended Masters, and those masters developing on Earth who are working toward your transformation and Ascension. Located in beautiful Hawaii, The Council of Light, Inc. offers Accelerated Transformation Programs of global proportion, and is actively developing masters worldwide.

The need for expanding Consciousness and Enlightenment is great, and will accelerate as we near the year 2,000. To accommodate our growing family of Light Workers the Council of Light, Inc. now has branch offices in: Honolulu—Hawaii, Mount Shasta—California, Los Angeles—California, Sedona—Arizona, Hong Kong, and Chiang Mai—Thailand.

INTRODUCTION TO THE ASCENDED MASTERS

By Bob Fickes
Spiritual Teacher, Shaman and Channel for the Masters

The Ascended Masters are universal teachers, Archangels, and enlightened Souls, who have completed their Earthly duties and karma, and ascended beyond Earth and its spirit realms into universal dimensions of Wisdom, Love, and Power—the three-fold Flame of Life!

The Ascended Masters offer assistance—radiating Spiritual Light and Insight into all that they do. Their discourses are filled with the power of Ascension and carry powerful radiations of spiritual energy to awaken your highest potential and spiritual mastery. The words that you will be reading in the following discourses are bridges from the Masters to you. They are living vibrational attunements that actually connect you to the dimension of your *I AM Presence* and take you to the home of all universal knowledge deep within your inner Divine Self! But even as you feast upon the mighty knowledge of systems both new and ancient provided for you in these teachings, you will most likely entertain many questions about the Ascended Masters and the Ascension Process.

In light of the fact that in the New Age community many divergent opinions exist about the Ascension Process—from the way out to the traditional—we are providing the following question and answer sequence to assist you. Putting the pieces together can become a difficult and confusing process. Here then is the view we have learned and experienced over the last two and one-half decades.

Q: Who are the Ascended Masters, where do they come from, why are they making themselves known to the citizens of Earth—now?

A: The Ascended Masters are a group of Beings that originally came from the Central Sun. They are divinely created and have travelled throughout the universe to assist evolving Souls at all levels. They have been participating with our solar system, and with our Earth for millions of years. All of the other planets in our solar system have ascended already. Every planet in our solar system has human life, but they are on a higher vibrational frequency and are not usually detected by our telescopes. They would be transparent to our vision because their molecular activity is faster than ours, and so we would be looking for something condensed and carbon based as we are, when these

Beings are more made of Light.

Earth is the last planet to go through the ascension process, and not only are all the other planets of the solar system waiting for us but all the other life forms of our galaxy are waiting for us. We are the last in a long link, and when we finally pass through the gate to Ascension then it will open an even larger gate for the rest of our solar system to pass through. Just as if there were a couple cells of our human body that were still filled with illness, the rest of our body would have to wait for that to be cleared before it would feel better.

The Ascended Masters originally came to this Earth and set up what has been called, in many parts of the globe, the great White Brotherhoods and Sisterhoods of Light, the school of Melchizadek, the Council of Elders, the Immortals, the Brotherhoods and Sisterhoods of Shamballa, etc..

Q: How long have the Ascended Masters been here on Earth, and what was their original purpose in coming?

A: Sanat Kumara came here two and one-half million years ago during the time of Lemuria to establish an order of Masters at Shamballa just above the present day Gobi Desert. At that time it was seen that the cultures of the Earth had disintegrated to a point where the traditions would not be honored or maintained properly, and impurities would begin to creep in. So it was determined that an order of

Masters should remain with the Earth at all times, in Light form, to ensure that whatever direction the people on this planet should decide to take there would be a Master that could visit them and assist them.

Each of the Masters, including Buddha, Muhammad, Jesus, Mother Mary, Socrates, Shankara, Lao Tsu, Kwan Yin, etc., were Masters from that order, who had incarnated with the specific purpose of highlighting for that culture their truths. And when that highlighting came, it would always come in terms of the language and understandings of the people for that time period and that culture. Although they used different languages for different time periods and different cultures, it was all one message.

And now, since the cultures of the Earth are reunifying it is very imperative that we also reunify the traditions, the traditional understandings, and although it may look to be that Buddhism is different from Christianity, and Christianity is different from Judaism, and Judaism is different from whatever, these are basic misconceptions when in fact all religions share similar truths, profound in nature. Part of this process is a re-establishment of how important the Goddess Power is, and the matriarchal cultures of the Earth, the native cultures, the Shaman cultures, the devas of the land. The Ascended Masters are a group of Beings whose responsibility it is to assist us in this process of re-understanding and in the past they have chosen to embody, to incarnate as a Master for that purpose.

Today they have chosen to work with those of us here. Many of us here have had an alliance with these Councils of Light, these orders of Masters, and we have also been working with them, and waiting for the right time to expose our real inner purpose. Like everything else, it has to be well timed. We have all been waiting for that timing to occur, and it is happening now. So, each of our roles are now finally unfolding, after many lifetimes of waiting, and it is our responsibility, as citizens of the Earth, to bring out the new teachings. The Masters are there to help us, but they are really putting it in our hands rather than doing it for us, or coming forth with new teachings, as they have done in the past.

Q: Will the Ascended Masters appear to us in Angelic form, and do they herald the "Second Coming" of Jesus the Christ?

A: It is our understanding there will be no "second coming", no avatars, the sort of thing that will come and save the Earth. They will come, in their Light Body forms when we are capable of seeing them. But to be capable of seeing them means that we must take full responsibility for our own evolution and spiritual growth, and evolve to that point where we are capable of seeing Light Body Souls. Then they will come and we will not look on them as our saviors, but as examples of the high standard of life that God originally intended for us.

The real meaning of the "Second Coming" is the

awakening of the Christ or *Meshiach* within. The great ancient Rabbi Maimonides once defined the Meshiach as all of Israel (the world) rising up to Heaven together. Oh yes—Jesus will come, and so will Buddha and the others. But not as saviors—they will come instead as teachers.

So, all that I have learned from the Masters is that they are here to assist us in achieving our own Power. But in many cases they begin to disappear from us when we put too much emphasis on them, and de-emphasize ourselves. When we start to deify them they immediately disappear in order for us to stand in our own Truth, and our own Power., and this is an act of kindness, even though we might not like it. In my own case, I have been waiting for a manifestation of one of the Masters just to have concrete proof that what I am channelling and receiving is real. But they tend to leave me on the edge, which means I always have to empower myself, and trust where I am going, rather than have someone else do it for me. While not as delicious on one level, it is much more reaffirming and strengthening on another. And so, that is who the Ascended Masters are.

Q: Are we human Beings of Earth evolving into Ascended Masters?

A: Many of us are Ascended Masters who have been in a cycle, or chain of events here on Earth for so long that we have forgotten, or had to put aside, our powers. So many of us are returning to our original status as Masters. Not all of humanity came from Ascended Masters. There are certain ones that have achieved that status of evolvement and are here to serve the Earth, very like myself, who have been here for so long but have not been able to use our full power until such time as now, when the Earth is ready. We are now in the process of rediscovery of our forgotten gifts.

There are others who are evolving into that status. The whole universe evolves all at the same time. I have heard of many Ascended Masters and certain Yogic Masters say that "when Creation came forth, all levels of Creation were there, from the one-celled amoeba to the highest pinnacle of enlightenment and everything in between—it came out *all* at once.

If you were to look at our planet right now, you would see very sophisticated civilizations and very primitive civilizations. Primitive civilizations have very few records, but it is silly to assume that there were only primitive Beings long ago that kept evolving up into higher forms. At the same time it is ridiculous to assume that primitive Beings will always remain primitive, no, they are always evolving, at all times. So there are Beings on Earth that are re-gaining their Ascended status, and there are Beings that are Ascended and staying in Light and assisting us from the unseen, and there are Beings who have yet to achieve that status from their own evolutionary status. All things can exist simultaneously—one does not cancel out the other.

Q: What is the fundamental difference between the Ascended Masters and Astral Teachers?

A: All Beings are a thought of God. And when Beings come out of God, or the Central Sun, it means God has a complete thought which will encompass everything in the universe it needs to complete that thought. From those who have to dig into the ground so that the foundation can be poured, to those who pour the foundation, to those who build the skyscraper up into the air, to those who would eventually inhabit it, and to those who would simply look at it. Whenever a thought of God comes out, it is *all* there. And it comes out *all* at the same moment, as a litter.

From God's perspective, those who dig into the ground, and those who inhabit the building are on equal status as they are just fulfilling the complete thought of God. The hierarchy we create. If you want to have some credence to hierarchy, we can tell you there are Beings who are more absorbed in their own inner Light and compassion, and are more loving and less restricted or restrained in their behavior, and if we wish to deify them or put them on a higher scale than ourselves, then that is appropriate, as they are living more of God's potential. But from their perspective they would never see themselves as higher than we are, and they are Ascended Masters.

Astral Beings will still have the band wagon to stand on, they will have a philosophy to promote, they will have do's and don'ts, rights and wrongs, and they will have some judgement associated with that. And so, whenever you hear someone preaching a little too hard, or *listen to me, you are doing it all wrong*, or they talk about struggle, believing *it will be difficult*, or of suffering—believing *it is necessary to suffer*, when in fact this is not the case, they are probably coming from an astral level that has not yet perceived the truth of this universe—*that all is one and everything is divinely achievable for every moment that we open our-selves to it.*

Q: The Ascended Masters—Jesus, Buddha, Kwan Yin, and the Merlin, to name only a few—refer to religious scriptures of every major religious belief on Earth—and in doing so obviate their strong similarities. Aren't in fact all religions basically the same, and don't most, if not all, religions share many of the same truths?

A: There are definite basic truths which I have noticed over my twenty-five years of spiritual growth and every few years, when I read different religious texts, I get more out of it. I am seeing things that I never knew were there because my inner vision and understanding has changed that much. I can remember twenty-five or thirty years ago when I was a child looking at, or even a teenager looking at, these scriptures and seeing how every religion looked different and how there were do's and don't's and moral codes and all that.

But one of the first misconceptions to go when I started along the path of spiritual growth and inner discovery, was the understanding that there were separate truths. I began to see the same truths. I became just as comfortable going to the Temple with my Jewish friends, or with my Hindu and

Buddhist friends, as I was in a church of Christ—it was all the same—and I was willing to open myself to that discovery. *As I began to open myself to that perspective, I began to realize that their differences in vocabulary were only differences in perspective that can help me to see a bigger perspective.*

Q: Is Ascension only for human Beings, or is it a quickening for all levels of Beings?

A: What is happening on planet Earth at this time is a collective vibration that includes every life form—animate and inanimate—for even inanimate forms are life forms. To clarify this we need to go back to an understanding of what is God? God is all Creation, and God is a living Being out of which comes the life force that we all participate in. Everywhere we look these things that we call inanimate may be inappropriate, for can we truly call the composition of lead, and gold, and silver in our own bodies inanimate. It is there to help compose our life matter, our living tissue, and it is all participating in conducting life energy, electric life current—for if it carries Life current, is it not alive?

So, everything in Creation is *alive*, and everything in Creation has consciousness, some consciousness that moves faster and some that moves slower. The slower consciousness doesn't speak to us, the faster consciousness, a human Being or an Angel, can speak and convey intelligence. Intelligence is just a display of creativity of energy. Slower energy is not quite as creative, it moves slower. Faster energy moves more creatively and expresses itself in a lot of different directions, it has more "intelligence."

The whole planet Earth at this time is absorbed in a frequency shift. The actual molecules of our planet have been rearranged already. This does not mean that the geometry has been rearranged, but it has been spread out. We are having more space between the molecules—they are not as compacted or condensed. It is happening now, because a thousand years ago we were more absorbed in ideologies and we compressed our essence by the way we thought. When you are trying to live according to philosophy you are always holding yourself back, and you will feel tight. And so, people on our planet have been "up tight."

We are up tight because we disallow ourselves to be who we are through restricted thought form, and this creates a tightness in our Being. When you start to emotionally relax, your whole Being is going to feel much more relaxed or spread out, which actually frees the molecular components, and over time it will create a shift. And when you have a certain number of those elements within a physical system relaxing there is a phase shift that occurs once you reach that number—it is actually mathematical. That phase shift in physics occurs when a certain percentage of the elements of a system are ready to go through the shift. Water will start to line up, and then at a certain point it becomes ice. There is a phase shift that takes place when a certain number of the molecules line up in a certain pattern and all of a sudden the water is frozen. That phase shift occurs at 32°

Fahrenheit.

So, the same thing is true with our Earth. We now have enough Souls, or consciousness, on our planet that have relaxed to shift the density of our planet. It is interesting when you look at densities of planets, because Earth is more dense than a planet like Jupiter, which is quite large.

Q: As we relax and move into Ascension—toward the Light—are we in fact re-enacting, or re-visiting, those earlier days of Atlantis or Lemuria?

A: Yes, we are re-tracing history as we go back and relax. The earlier history of our Earth was actually more advanced, and in fact much of the technology coming to Earth at this time from our space brotherhood, particularly the Pleiadians, is knowledge that is being returned to us that we originally taught to them. Long ago, we were more advanced than those space civilizations are today, and as we return to our original perception we will retain that original knowledge.

There are places on the Earth where that knowledge is actually hidden in caves, and waiting to be discovered. There are references to these places in every mystical tradition on Earth—the Buddhists talk about it, the Hindus talk about it, the Christians talk about it, and within the metaphysical circles such as the traditions of Egypt, they all refer to certain caves that carry ancient knowledge.

Q: How did we fall from Grace, and turn away from our original condition—our Light Form—condensing our bodies?

A: This is covered more thoroughly within this text, but briefly what happened was, we were originally created in what the Biblical tradition calls the "Garden of Eden." And the Garden was a Garden of life where we could do anything we wanted, and have anything we wanted—God gave us it all. And He said the only thing that He recommended that we not do was taste of the fruit of the tree of good and evil.

What that literally means is that as soon as we started to taste what it means to be good or evil, we created limitations in that Garden. For the Garden was there for our pleasure, and we could do anything we wanted in it, but if we started to call one thing "good" and the other thing "evil" then we just created a limitation that said we can only do the good things and not the evil things, and after a while even the good things would have shades of gray. And under certain circumstances, even a good thing could be considered an evil thing. Thus, after a while we created so much limitation in life and as I mentioned earlier, we walked around feeling "up tight", literally creating our limitations to the point that we created physical form which eventually reduced the life span.

They say that in Lemuria the life span was one million years. Early Atlantis, about one hundred thousand, and later Atlantis was about ten thousand, and just after the fall of

Atlantis about a thousand years. In fact, in many traditions, including our own Bible, they talk about people who lived almost a thousand years or several hundreds of years, etc. And the long and the short of it is that we have shortened our life-span now to barely one hundred years because of our thought forms that prevent us from living the truth of life, which is unlimited flow. So we are re-tracing, or going back.

The key to that retracing is, as they say throughout the following text, in nearly every chapter, is releasing our judgements and our thought forms and allowing ourselves to "be natural" and to follow our heart, and the higher instincts through our heart and not through the mind as much—and that leads to Ascension. Ascension is what happens when you no longer put a vice grip on your emotions and spiritual personality. When you let that relax, the next process is a shift and we start to "space out" or spread out, expand our consciousness, and our Being. We are able to become less dense where we can eventually float through the sky, just like in our dreams. We can do that, when the body becomes light enough. We can walk through matter. All the things that children think that they can do— and then learn that they have physical bodies that are denser than that. But children come in knowing the Soul is capable of doing it, and then are trained to adjust when their body cannot do it. Yogi's in India, however, have practiced techniques enabling them to do these things for the past several thousand years.

Q: Must we die physically to Ascend? What changes will occur for ourselves and the planet Earth?

A: No—Ascension is something that is very natural. And it certainly does not mean that we have to leave this Earth, or leave the physical body to achieve it. It means that everything on Earth has to go through this phase shift, including the rocks, the homes, the cars, everything. And when we go into Ascension it is not going to mean that we no longer have homes and cars and food and those things, we still will have an appetite for the things that we create. That is not going to just disappear, but it will all be on a higher frequency.

Q: Will human life cease to exist as we know it, and does our Life Force go off into space—somewhere?

A: Even when you are Ascended and enlightened you still enjoy playing and creating. If you like to cook, you always want to get a little more creative with your cooking. Creativity doesn't stop just because you have Ascended.

And so now that we have cleared up the image that some people have who feel that you have to die and have your body change. We have cleared up the idea that when you Ascend you are going to go off into space somewhere. You do not go off into space.

Just leaving this planet doesn't change our planet, and as Merlin once put it: " it leaves a garbage heap behind." I can tell you as one with expanded vision who sees throughout the universe, no matter where you go, you are going to know you left a garbage heap behind. And you will still feel that as part of your Being, and your nature will be to heal it, and to clear it.

Merlin once showed me a great vision of someone who went from the Earth, through the door into what they thought was Heaven, only to find they were right back on Earth again, and looking around and asking: "what happened. I just thought I went into Heaven, and here I am back on Earth." And so they go back through the door again to find that Earth is on both sides of the door, and that what they thought was Heaven is just Earth transformed. In fact, what they say in the *Book of Revelations* is a new Heaven and a new Earth. That doesn't mean that the old one was destroyed, it just means that our new vision changes the way we see things and the way we see the divinity in life. Right now, we are in a decade (the '90's) in which a main phase shift is occurring from third dimension into fourth dimension.

Q: What is our time frame for the Ascension process, and where are we (citizens of Earth) presently in the cycle?

A: From the year 2,000, particularly around the year 2,010, within the next twenty years, there will be a major phase shift. The Masters have often referred to 1995 as a major turning point. This is not something that just happened in the '90's, neither did it just happen in the '80's or the '70's. It has been happening for a long time. There are those who are awake early in the morning, and they get to see the birds come out and sing. Others are sleeping when the birds are singing. If you are asleep when the birds are singing, and someone tells you that "you know, early in the morning the birds sing" you will call them a liar. It all depends on whether you are awake or not.

With every new shift, particularly when you look at the last two hundred years, you will see that prior to every scientific discovery there were spiritualists that had perceived those same principles, but from a more esoteric perspective. Then later, someone would be able to bring it into physical concrete form and make a science of it. And you will see this prior to World War II, World War I, and prior to the Industrial Revolution. You will see major shifts in consciousness, first in the spiritual community and then later something manifesting more concretely in society. There will be those who are more sensitive, and they are called "sensitives", that perceive these things before everybody else does. This is also true of people like Einstein who knew the theory of relativity before he could prove the mathematics of it. And Edison, who knew that the light bulb was a real phenomenon, which is why he was not discouraged after two hundred tries. He knew these were just two hundred ways, as he puts it, that didn't work. But he knew that the principle of the light bulb existed. How did he know that? He had a perception of reality.

So now, for the last 2,000 years since Jesus demonstrated the resurrection process, which was to be a living memory, not just for Christians, but for people all over the world, wherein we have been shown a principle whereby the body can be transmuted and come back to life, and be lifted into a higher element of Light. That image was to be there for these two thousand years when the planet would be moving toward the year 2,000 and getting ready for collective Ascension.

The second coming is not one man, it is the coming of a collective vibration of the Christ consciousness. Christ Consciousness, is a term used throughout these teachings in a very general sense. I am not referring to the Master Jesus when I say Christ Consciousness, but to a consciousness that could also be called Buddha consciousness, or Hindu consciousness. Whatever the language it means we will all have compassion and respect for our fellow man, woman, child, and any living thing of Earth and the body of Earth herself. If we do not achieve this level of understanding of the body of Earth by the year 2,000, there are many scientists on our planet who say that biological life on our planet cannot continue, either because the ozone layer will get us, or the pollution will get us—there are so many factors now that are right on the brink, that may even push us into an ice age. And these scientists are not quacks, they are very serious and have been investigating this for a long time. They are brilliant people who are all, from their various perspectives, saying this. We need to change, as a planet, to survive. And, this is what *is* going to happen, and has been planned for 2,000 years and longer.

Q: Why is the year 2,000 believed to be a crucial turning point (time period) for human Beings, and all citizens of Earth, in the Ascension process?

A: We are actually completing a two and one-half million year cycle that started with Sanat Kumara, also known as "the Ancient of Days", "the Ancient One", etc. We are completing a two thousand year cycle that began with the Masters Jesus, Buddha, Socrates, Lao Tsu, and Shankara. We are also completing a smaller cycle of about one hundred and fifty years, and a cycle now of a ten year time period where we are kind of in between. And so this "day" as the Masters put it, of this decade (a decade is a day in time) is going to be composed of two halves.

The first half, or as the Light gets brighter, is similar to having a dark room and when you turn the light on, the first thing that you see is the mess that you've made in the dark. *So, the first half of this decade is going to be looking at the mess. The second half of the decade will be cleaning it up.* And after that process is complete there should be very few resistances left to the whole planet ascending and going into Light. In that time period there will be waves of people going into this phase of Light together. But, again, they will not leave the planet but will remain here to assist.

Some of them may want to rest because they have been working for a long time. But I am seeing many of those who thought they were going to leave to rest deciding that they are going to be here. As one who is committed to the Earth, it has been my feeling all along that we are all going to be staying here and doing our work, none of us are going to leave until it is done. We are so close—why leave! A few more seconds in time won't matter. And those few seconds will be worth sticking around to see the fruits of our work.

So this period will take us from third dimension into fourth dimension. Fourth dimension experience, as covered in these teachings, means we will feel lighter, there will be no friction, because we will not have thought interference or ideology interference. We will trust our insight, we will trust our motives, we will have complete faith in our Being and we will act on that—that is fourth dimension. We will feel as though we are transparent Beings, and when we look down at our own physical body there will be a transparency about it that we will feel and see for ourselves. But when we look in the mirror and when others look upon us we will still appear to be physical with the same ideas and attitudes that we have had before.

When we emerge into the fifth dimension, which is another two thousand year sequence, then to someone in the third dimension we will be completely transparent and not physical. Like our brothers and sisters on other planets who are mostly fifth dimension Beings or more, we will not be visible to third dimensional eyes. That vibration is the same as the fourth because it has no friction. We will have a lot of the same attitudes and ideas, but they will be even more refined and more filled with Love. The difference between the fourth dimension and the fifth dimension can be one of godliness, or loveliness. We will become more beautiful as Beings. We will have more capacities both to love and be loved, and do things and create things. Fifth dimensional Beings also have the power of physical manifestation through thought form and heart form, and so all the spiritual powers will be available to us also.

There will be many Masters on this planet after the year 2,000 who will ascend into the fifth dimension. When the whole planet is fourth dimensional they will be able to see fifth dimensional Beings like Jesus, Saint Germain, Buddha, etc. The Masters Jesus, Maitreya, Saint Germain, etc., will not need to be "born on Earth" as many suggest. They will come in their fifth dimensional forms, so we can learn from them about the Enlightened Way of Life. They have no need to further teach about third dimensional experience.

When you die, you remain in the third dimension, normally. Astral Beings are considered by the Masters to be in the third dimension. Even though sometimes we do not physically see them, that is again because of our limited perception. There are many people in the third dimension who are called psychic who can see them, even children can see them. It is a part of our third dimensional reality, and astral spirits, even spirit teachers, are really no more enlightened than we are except that they do not have bodies. Their Souls are the same as our Souls, with the exception they are free of a body and we are not. That means, when they look around they do not have the four walls of their house to block their view.

Q: So then, you are saying that astral and physical Beings co-exist in the third dimension, but not necessarily on the physical plane?

A: Yes—there are ten billion Souls that have been associated with Earth, and at different periods in history there have been more or less of them who have been physically embodied, which accounts for the differences in populations. But now because more and more Souls on the other side are wanting to ascend and evolve beyond physicalness into godliness, there are more who are taking embodiment, hence, a population boom!

Traditionally it is understood by all metaphysical circles and in every tradition in the world that you do not evolve in an astral body. That, basically, you are on vacation until you get back into a physical body where you can evolve and change your karma. The astral period in between bodies is more like a review period where you are allowed to review your life and prepare your next one. Or, just have a vacation. But when you are ready to actually deal with your karma again, the weight of karma takes you into a physical form. And it is actually a weight, it is thought form that condenses your personality once again into a physical matter.

Q: Is physical immortality both a fourth and fifth

dimensional reality?

A: Yes—anything other than the third, as third is the only one that participates in death. It is also the only one that participates in sleep. You do not sleep and you do not die in fourth dimension and above. Every Being from fourth dimension and upwards is conscious of their infinity. They have already merged their essence with God. The only difference is in the rate of vibration of the form in which they dwell, but their consciousness is one with infinity. And when you finally merge your form with your infinite consciousness, completely one hundred percent, then there is no longer any reason for being separate from God—you are no longer separate from God and the Central Sun.

Another way of looking at it is that some thoughts that you have will sustain you throughout your entire lifetime. You will constantly be delighted every time you participate in that thought. Other thought forms only have enough juice behind them to interest you once. What that means is that everything is just a thought form of God, so there are some activities that God creates that will last throughout the whole Creation. There are other activities that God creates that will only last for one particular purpose, and that is it. Certain Masters came to our planet for one purpose, and that was it—they were finished. If historians are correct then Jesus only taught for three years, during which time he completed his mission here on Earth. Everything we now know of as Christianity was taught in three years, which is not a very long time, but he had a very powerful purpose and a very powerful intention, and achieved very powerful results.

Another Master would possibly have taught for a longer period, although even Buddha did not teach for that long—maybe fifteen years or so. Some historians say forty, but I believe we can safely say it was a much lesser time period during which he taught from his *enlightened* perspective. Then there are other Masters whose purposes were different. They were bound to different traditions.

Babaji, for instance, the immortal Yogi Christ of India, has been said to be around for thousands of years. People who have seen him throughout the last few centuries have always reported and described him in the same way. He is also said to have been the teacher of Shankara, also to have taught Buddha, and to have had meetings with Jesus, and in fact to have been a close companion of his. Now, this is a Master who has been around a long time, but you don't really hear his name, because that really isn't his purpose. He didn't have that intense focus that Jesus, or Buddha, or Shankara had. But on the other hand, his mission in terms of his physical form and identity on Earth, was to have existed for a long time and achieve physical immortality. When we refer to physical immortality, we refer to anything fourth dimensional and beyond. There are many ways in which you can slice infinity and still be infinite.

A lot of what we understand now is quantum mechanics, quantum field theory, the theory of the vacuum state, superfluidity and superconductivity. Many qualities such as levitation and manifestation can also be achieved in third dimension, but a Being may only be able to achieve one or two of these powers.

In fourth dimension you would have all of these qualities as a natural ability, anything that you want. Although in fourth dimension you still would probably have to be shown how to do it, what the mechanics are, while in fifth dimension it would be a spontaneous occurrence. All of those abilities would be natural phenomenon. Everybody will be flying through the air in fifth dimension. In fourth dimension you would have to see someone do it, and then once that you see it can be done, you will believe you can do it.

And that is also why the Masters will come again to Earth, like Jesus and the others that have Ascended. They will not be born, but will just come as they are and show us what life can be like in higher dimensions. As we see it then we will learn from that. That is the only reason for them to come, to show us how to polish or refine the fourth dimension. And when will they come? After the year 2.000, around the year 2,010. Although, all time tables are dependent on our free will, and our choices. If we make all the choices the way it is scheduled, we may achieve it earlier than the year 2,000. That is up to us, and there are people here who are dragging their feet. We tend to wait until we are shoved—to change— and even those of us who know better still hold on to a lot.

There are so many idea forms that we still hold on to no

matter how wise we are, and until we let go of all of them, and let go of them collectively, we will not be completely in the fourth dimension, let alone the fifth.

And so, let us begin our wondrous journey and lead you from the third dimension—toward the Light—into Ascension—<u>for the time has come ...</u>

These teachings are the first in a series of combined discourses on Ascension from the Realm of Spiritual Teachers and Ascended Masters Æolus, Ezekiel, Sananda (Jesus the Christ), and the Merlin as well as Lady Masters Pallas Athena, Mother Mary, and Kwan Yin. The powerfully moving information contained herein will impart untold knowledge of systems both new and ancient, of Heaven and of Earth, to assist you on your endlessly fascinating and exciting journey of self-discovery and personal understanding—a gift of love from the Masters to all of mankind. It is not meant to emphasize the Ascended Masters themselves, but to develop the Master within each of you. Blessings to you ...

Om Selah!
(all there is, and all there can be!)

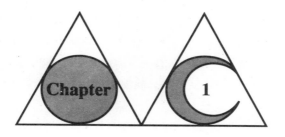

WHAT IS ASCENSION: A QUICKENING

By Ascended Master Æolus and Lady Master Pallas Athena

To all . . . blessings. And peace to you. I am Pallas Athena, together with my divine complement Æolus, we greet you. And we bring you Power . . . and we bring you Light . . . and we bring you Love. Rest in that love now, and be assured that all that which is about to occur, shall occur within you, and shall accelerate that which you are, into a new dimension of Being.

This Being is to unfold upon the Earth in all of its greatness, and all of its beauty. It is truly the flowering of the Earth to all possibilities. It is the creation of a new dimension and perception of Earth and all surrounding communities. It is the alignment and the alliance of all the particle cells of God's body of light. And this body of light is to descend into the Earth and to lift the Earth out of its misery into hope in Heaven—into peace and goodwill—into harmony with all living things, and with all creation.

Therefore, we greet you with great love, great understanding and wisdom, and great peace. And we surround you with this love now. May you be enveloped by it, and may the body in which you currently dwell be affected by it. Close your eyes and be at peace. For this is a transmission of deep inner peace. It is a frequency of light that is more subtle and yet more grand than any perception you have ever held in this physical form.

You will remember it, however, from long ago when you were perfect. When you were yet breathing the life of God with every breath. When you understood the concept and the condition of all life being a part of God, and when there was no division among you. Into this place of perfection we lead you, for it is a memory, and it is a re-awakening of olden times—of times long ago. Of a time in which all was perfect and in balance.

May this Light envelope you and fill you with
the deepest most abiding Love.
And may its Grace pervade every system in the
body, every cell in the body.
And may the body be feeling this Light as a
liquid, with great penetrating qualities.

And may your Selves drink of that liquid and
know it as its *soma*, as its nectar divine.
And may this Light nourish every element of
the body, and may it be filled with Love.

Drink the nectar slowly, dear ones, as it is poured
forth to each of you. And may your bodies settle into the
Light and merge with it. Out of this Light you have come,
and to this Light you return. And all Earthly forms shall
drink of the Light until such time as it becomes it. Then it
drinks the nectar eternally, for the nectar is eternally produced.
It is the offspring of your perception, it is the harmony of the
divine senses. And as these senses become divine, they
drink the nectar with each perception. For each perception
becomes one of Love. All things become of a likeable
condition, an eternal moment of pleasantness. And the
perceptions increase, and become more divine until all of
this—all that is—is a part of them.

And they drink of the nectar of their own divineness
that exists everywhere. Out of all of existence comes forth
Light for at the basis of all existence is Light. So it is around
you, so it is within you. So it is beyond you, and so it is
within your reach. It is everywhere. Never is there a place
where light cannot be found, truly. For even in the darkness
there is light, though it remains hidden from your view.

Open then those eyes that would perceive it. Experience then the pleasantness and the joy, and let this then
come to you peacefully for in a moment you shall be filled

with all of it as it is your divine gift from Heaven. We ask you then, dearest Children of Light, to receive this gift with open arms. And may these arms be arms of Light coming forth from each cell.

> See each cell then, reaching forth for the divine
>   and drinking of this nectar.
> See each cell of the body with open arms re-
>   ceiving it.
> See the cup runneth over.
> Let Goodness and Joy, Light and Love, pervade
>   you in every way.

This then, dear ones, is the acceleration of your Being. A tangibleness of your own dimension begins to melt with this divine nectar. This is the divine nectar of Heaven. It is Heaven's door. It is given to you each day for you to enjoy. And yet we see you upon the Earth without this nectar, as though it did not exist. We see your senses bombarded with perceptions that bring you other than joy— they bring you weight, and condition—they bring you separation and form. And these perceptions you carry with you daily, and they mount upon one another until they become heavy with burden.

And your bodies are filled with such burdens as have been passed to you by your ancestors, and your perceptions have become clouded and weary. And those things that you have become on Earth have become the best of you, for that which truly rests in Heaven remains silent and behind the door which was closed.

But now we open the door unto you, and to every cell of your Being. And the floodlights reach through the darkness until they reach your cells. The cells of your Being created by your own essence. We ask you now to be at peace with this Light, to be at peace with yourself, and to relax deeply into a meditation of the purest Light, the purest Love, and the purest Peace. To let go [of] the weariness, and the weight. To return it to the world in which it was given to you. And to allow that which you are, to rest inside, and to wait patiently.

> There is nothing to be done to create Ascen-
> sion—other than this:
> Releasing your burdens.
> Releasing those self proclaimed responsibili-
> ties.
> Releasing that which you are on Earth, to become
> come that which you are in Heaven, is
> the only condition for Ascension.

The body knows what to do, how to get there, what functions it must correct, what conditions it must overcome, what particle forms of belief must be released or corrected. All of this we can say in summary is a function of the Light of perception. And, therefore, it is to perception that we must return, with you in hand. And so we take you by the hand of the heart, and by the tiny hands of every cell, and we lead you into that dimension of truth where the nectar of love flows freely. And we ask you to relax. And to be in the stream of this nectar, and to float in it, and to float freely now. Let all of that perception of the world in which you have existed fade as if in a dream that occurred in the night. Place it behind you now, that the dream may be in appearance only a dream that has been.

And call upon that force that dwells within you, the mighty *I AM Presence*, and welcome it as the throne of your Being, the *Merkavah*. It is your senses that return to you, for you are both lord and ruler over them. And it is you who must command them. But a loving and gentle leader commands not with force and control, but with love and willingness to receive. Through the giving of love, and to the receiving of gifts, the senses would open to you. And all of your perceptions would become divine.

It is through this instinct of divine perception that this occurs. For this was the instinct given to each of your senses to pursue truth—lovingly and joyfully. Their innate direction would be in the flow of love. In the flow of greater perception. As they would drink of the nectar of life and receive of it as its nourishment. For that which you call perception of life, is the nourishment of the senses. And they would feed your senses, and they would become a part of you. For indeed the sense channeled itself as a bridge between you and all else that eventually becomes one with no bridge. Where you identify, merges with all of creation, and thusly with all of God and all that God is. For you were so given Life.

Borne out of the birthplace of the Creator.
In the same manner and condition as the Cre-
    ator, which was unlimited [and] is, and
    always shall be, perfection—unlimited
    and divine.
And this thou art.
And this thou shalt always be.
And this, my friends, thou art becoming, even
    now.

In this way then we ask you again to relax. And to receive the vision of home. Home is where the heart is and all things are placed therein around you. And this is where the throne is, for the throne of God dwells within you. In the seat of the heart, in the very center—is God. The mighty *I AM Presence* is God's representative. And you are a flame of God. A part of His very body. And with each intention that God would have as He dwells in Heaven, you would also have as you dwell on Earth. For the chamber of the heart is a multidimensional one, and stretches beyond all regions of perception. It lifts you into the realm and the teaching of God. And there you are at peace, for you go beyond your own Earthly condition.

All of this is a part of God, and every cell of your body [is] God's to command. And as you surrender into this pureness of existence, you surrender into your own divine Self within the heart, and to the center of your very Being. Your perception begins to change, and to alter your very environment in which you live. And there the condition becomes the Conditionless, and the limited becomes the Limitless. And all that *Is*—is of love, and of divine nectar—that you are drinking. And the center of your Being begins to grow and to spread—to spread all around you. And the senses of your Being create a bridge to bring forth out of the darkness the Light, until Light alone *Is*.

And in this wakefulness, there is a new Being emerging, or a new sense of that Being that you are, and have been all along. And it is familiar to you because it is of peace and of love. It is familiar in that it dwells in the heart, and is intimate to you. It is familiar for it is one who both loves, and eternally receives love as a part of its innate condition. It is not dependent upon its actions to receive this love or approval, but depends only on itself. And the fullness of its condition in life exists already. And this heart is strong and communicates its strength—its knowingness . . . its Beingness . . . and its oneness—to all parts of itself in the body.

And we ask you now as you sit upon the throne, to transform that which you are into Light, and to share this Light with all of your body and all parts of you. And this creates a *quickening*. Even as we say the words, [and ask you] to share the Light with all parts of you—you feel a sense of lightness, an acceleration of your Being, from the denseness that you were.

And let this Light carry you, and let it transform your Being from one of hardness to one of fluidity, and from the fluidity to pure space. For God is spacious and His mansion awaits you. And there you dwell, with all space around you and perfection in your very heart. And the breath of God flows through you, up and down your spine, and it brings living light and the nectar to nourish every cell. And every meridian is open to you, and every pathway. And those pathways become like rivers, out of rivulets. The nectar which once dripped from Heaven as a tiny raindrop of light now flows in rivulets, in streams, and in waters, becoming abundant until the rivers of life pulse through you. And to every cell, the river of life flows and there is a quickening.

A quickening is the spark of Life. It is the release of Life Force from its captivity. It is the Conditionless life, for it is the condition that captivated it in the first place. And as the Conditionless is removed from its hiding place, it begins to flow and to quicken. It increases its space with excitement, as it anticipates its return to God and to Heaven. And Heaven's doors are all open wide to it, for there is much space in Heaven. And none of you can fill it. And yet all of you are Full with it. And there is always more to go, and more to share, and the Light is eternal, and the bridges of the senses shall spread eternally. And they shall form a loop within your Being, as they bring it all home, and home is where the heart is. For the senses drink their perceptions, and they are a nectar of God. And this nectar shall fill the senses. And the loop shall be completed. As the sense perception is drawn into the home, into the heart, and to dwell therein. And bring exhilaration, and freedom, and wisdom, and bliss.

For in truth, dear ones, as your senses properly
      perceive, all is the nectar of Life.
And all is of Love.
And all is of Wisdom, and Intelligence, and
      Understanding.
And your senses would delight in this, and
      they would drink of it eternally—would
      you only permit them.

How often your conditions return, and return to you
again and again and again. But in this moment, there is a
challenge, and the challenge comes on toward [you] by your
own creation. And it is out of your freedom that you have
willed it to be so. It is also out of your training, and your
habit. And as you would do so, we would ask of you, to
release this freedom into Light. And to live this freedom
eternally, as a bird would spread its wings. And to spread its
wings through Heaven's door, and feel the senses drink its
nectar. For the senses are that which is divine within you and
they would drink of these things, and you would know them,
and they would not be separate from you but a part of you—
a living Light—a life that is of One. For you are of One, and
there is no other. And all of this that has appeared separate
from you, is truly a part of you, and you have controlled it,
and you have organized it, and you have placed it before
you. What to do with it—but release it.

And know that it will not be lost or taken from you
unless it is God's will, and whatsoever is God's will is the
divine in you, and shall accelerate your perceptions. And

that which was removed will be replaced. For all things come and go, and all things would come to you as you require them. This is the knowledge of the senses, and the task of direct perception. *For direct perception is like a bridge to connect you to the divine in all things.* Hungrily your senses will drink in their own perceptions, and hungrily the heart will receive them. And this hunger *is* the quickening.

All things speed up as they are liberated. The life within a seed begins to stir, before the seed would sprout. And the heart *is* like a seed, and it *is* sprouting now. And its sprouts are the sense perceptions as they travel outwards through the body from the heart. And they are the rivers of life. And they drink the nectar and are in search of still more nectar. See the rivulets of life as golden light extending from the heart center. From the mighty *I AM Presence* at the very core of the heart, the rivulets of life, of golden light, sprout forth.

And see them first in your own heart center with a quickening of love, and a warmth and glow, as a Central Sun within you. The core atom of your existence, the *I AM Presence*, begins to glow. And see the electricity of that atom now as rivulets of energy and liquid light, a golden light. Fragmenting itself in all directions, but not separating—like the branches of a tree. And this is the tree of life, and it is the nectar, and the nectar is sweet.

But the Tree of Life, that stands at the center of

the Garden, has a warning associated
with it.
And that is never to taste the fruit of good and
evil.
For within all sense perception is the knowledge and condition that you might place
upon it.

For it is you that are Conditionless. And it is your
sense perceptions that would place conditions upon you. It
is up to you, as the nectar of life flows, and as the position
of life moves, to be free with it. And what is that condition?
It is the condition that would stop the flow and wish to hold.
So whenever you would feel a grasping motion, let go of it,
and let the rivers of life flow, and let the tree of life grow, and
let it spread its branches into all places.

And all things of Heaven and all things of
Earth shall come to rest under its
branches.
And these things shall be made known to you
without your asking.
For immediate are the gifts of Heaven.
Slow are they from Earth.

For on Earth you would hold too tightly, and you
would strangle the life out of them. And you would create
a field of suspension, which you call death.

Death is the illusion of the sense perception, created when the River of Life no longer flows.

Once the River of Life has ceased to flow, the life will become boring and lifeless. It would cease to satisfy, and its very warning is pain and suffering, disillusionment, and lack of freedom. Condition has been placed on that which wants to flow eternally.

The River of Life, the Tree of Life, are all God's perceptions. And they know automatically where they are to go. When you control them, you stop their motion and you strangle them. In the quietness and peace of your heart, you know this. And yet you are afraid. For fear is borne of control, and lack of freedom. And so, dear ones, you have dwelt in a condition, without freedom, for as long as the mind can count. For so long as the mind has been counting, you have conditioned life, and have hardened it.

What was once free and filled with Light, and
    spread everywhere, you have narrowed.
And you have chosen form over formless, and
    freedom.
And you have chosen control over natural, and
    liberated.
And you have chosen death and sleep, over life
    and rest.

For there is no true rest in death, or in sleep. For this is merely a condition to release the nervousness of life. And the nervousness of life is the jitter under the control. You may have seen with your automobiles how the engine will rear up as you accelerate with one foot, and brake with the other. And how the very machinery begins to shake. And were you not careful with that machinery, it would break, as the pressure becomes too great within it to accelerate forward on one hand, and to restrain back with the other.

And now you understand the root cause of all illness in the body. It begins with the driver, and not with the condition of the vehicle. For the vehicle was created out of perfection, out of Light. And the Tree of Life grew until it had many branches and bore fruit. And the Rivers of Light, your senses, reached forth for greater knowledge, but began to define itself by that knowledge, and hold fast to those conditions. And as your senses held fast, then that which was the acceleration of your Being was slowed down. And you contracted of your essence, and you froze of your forms. And you were no longer willing to expand and to travel, but to create the illusion—to stay in one place, in one form.

But your senses knew they could not do this, for life continues moving. *The very essence of life is motion.* And though it stems from the motionless eternal quality of God, it is the motion that fills itself that is called *Life*. The motion that fills the Motionless. For what you call Motionless, the motionless silence and peace that you achieve in your meditation, is in reality constantly moving, but out of that which is a superfluid condition, free of friction, there is no resistance in it.

You have defined all motionlessness as silence. And yet we say to you that silence is active. And that motionlessness has motion. But it has no friction. And this is why Ascension is called *a quickening*. For a quickening is a natural condition of life, it is the motion within the Self, it is the motion of the Motionless—free of friction. For life is eternally growing, and expanding. And the Tree of Life will spread its branches, to shelter and to bring love, and to bring fruit to all Beings.

Let go then of those things that you are, in definition and control, and allow yourself to be all that you are as you continue to expand and to grow. Be not afraid of those things that you would let go, that you might lose them. *But to know that there is no loss in Heaven, only a gain of something new.* This [quickening] the sense perceptions will survive, and those things which they love will be brought to them. For this is the eternal commandment of God. Even as He created all of this creation, this was His eternal commandment, and this is good, and this is great. And this is a blessing of Life.

> And thus God created [the Heaven and the Earth] on one day, and saw that it was good.
> And in the seven days God created Life, and saw that it was good.
> And there were seven chambers of the heart.
> And seven senses of the perception.
> And each of those chambers were then placed

on the Staff of Life—the Tree of Life—
and they were called the *sephiroth*.

They were called the Heavenly chakras and wheels.
And with each wheel, life was driven to a new destination,
to a new achievement, and to a new spiritual reality.

And all seven wheels turned evenly and at the same
pace, and they were all liquid in nature, and held no friction
within them. And they were free. Even now, as your sense
perceptions become enlivened, those wheels that have become rusted with age, and with control, [and] with restraint,
are now beginning to move freely and they are turning, they
are spinning. Your Earthly chakras are mirrors of those
which exist in Heaven, wheels within wheels, spins within
spins. And each dimension has its wheels, and its chakra
systems. And all are alike and unique at the same time. For
they are all borne out of the same essence—out of your
essence.

And with each perception there is uniqueness and
spreading, and there is wisdom, and there is joy. And those
senses then, would travel through the body, one sense at a
time. Each chamber of the body becomes filled with them,
and with their light. And there are many bodies you see.

For each dimension there is a perception.
And for each perception there is a perception
     vehicle, a sense vehicle.
And for each vehicle there is a river, a river of

Life flowing.
And you have condensed of your forms into
    physical matter.
And this physical matter knows only itself as
    physical.
And knows not its other conditions, but is
    learning them.

Learn the Wisdom of Life, and the Freedom of Life, and the sense perceptions will be opened unto you. And those things which would flow inside of you, would flow of God. And the life force will return to you. Just as the rear gate of a great and magnificent dam would be lifted, and the water from it flow throughout all of the fields which were once dry.

And now, breathe forth, and live in this Light of Freedom. That all of your crops might grow and be abundant. Do not be afraid, if at first when the rivers flow, [for] that which has become dried and hardened will become soft. And that some of that which is its mud will be washed away. Do not fear these things of change, for they are part of life, and life is now growing, again.

And when your seeds—your desires, your thoughts, and your feelings—are touched by the River of Life, let them grow, and let them grow freely. And honor that which is your Giver in Heaven, and to know that to be a part of you. And that part of you knows its ultimate direction. And each thing that is of your Soul, that is made of your Soul, will change and transform into Light. And *this* is Ascension, and *this* is the transition that you call *a quickening*.

The acceleration of life shall spread in all directions, and into all forms, and into all feeling, and heal them. A wound is that which is a gaping hole, created by the separation and pulling apart of your senses from their goals. It is like the sense reaching forward, and your pulling it back. Creating a hole—a wound. And this wound now must fill itself and heal. Healing then is the mending of the wound, the closing of the hole—of separation. This is why we have used the term *bridge of the senses*. That you might truly understand that the gateway has a bridge to connect you to those things that you want. And you want perfect freedom to experience them.

Blessings to you, dear ones, for you are now
perceiving greatly!

In the beginning, your senses were limited, and they were challenged with our words. But now they carry grace, they no longer resist, and their actions are smooth and graceful. God possesses you now, even as He did in the beginning. He is both your loving Father and Mother, for you are *all* His children. And therein lies the secret of life. That you are His children—His offspring. That which has sprung forth out of His own Being.

It is His Rivers of Life that move through you,
and your sense canals.

It is His Rivers of Life which nurture your
    crops, and fill your fields with water.
And you and your mind and intellect are its
    rear gates, and its deceivers.
And it is you that have learned to control
    existence, and restrain its flow.
Now—let thy Life be unlimited and let thy
    senses be divine.
And recognize the God in you.
And give Him a place of honor, at the very
    center of your hearts.

We ask you now, dear hearts, to release for but a
moment, and to share love. This with yourself, and your
own divine nature. Blessings to you ...

And so we begin.
And so all of life begins, and then the transition
    begins with it.
And those soils which have been hardened and
    dried, become lubricated.
And the quickening process continues.

I am Æolus, with Pallas Athena, and we welcome you
once again to a quickening of life in the third dimension.
Through each of its transformations and healings, in the
other dimensions.

And what begins, is a trickle of water into a dry and
dusty field. And as that water begins to flow, the field would

feel it. It would be as though something opens up from deep within you, and a new perception is given to you. With each perception, there is as though a thrill, a quickening, an acceleration of Life Force, the motion of the water through the sense canal to the dry field.

And with this then, we must learn to recognize that though the water be pure when it starts, as it touches the dry and dusty field, it becomes filled with the dust particles. And this is called the transition of the human Spirit, and the Soul as it forms itself into a new body, into a new sense perception, into a fertile ground. For your ground was once fertile, but has dried up as a result of your own conditions upon your senses, and upon their perceptions.

Now, as you learn to open the windows of perception and embody that which you are, the senses themselves will open the gates.

And the water and nectar of God will pour
forth.
And it pours into a dry and empty field.
And there the dust will move.
And the particle forms of previous existence,
of all the manners in which life has dried
up, will now become nourished.
And those things which you have pushed out
of place, and into what you have thought
to be your place, will now be moved.
And there will be faced many challenges.

As the field itself becomes rearranged.
The dust particles moved from one place to
    another, as the stream would have it
    flow.

Allow your senses to reorganize your life, and to do so patiently. There is no hastening to this process, for only so much can be done without harm or injury to self. For indeed, were the gates to be opened all at once, your field would be flooded, and all would be an untimely mess.

And so it is that the divine works, mysteriously and gradually—peacefully. That those things that would come to you would come to you as a result of what the divine in you would will. And the divine is always compassionate, and filled with love. It will never bring you more than what you are able to handle. Do not control the flow of life. Do not force your will. But allow that to unfold patiently out of this deep inner peace, and this deep inner contentment. You will find that your fields will flourish more rapidly than you expect. And the challenges of life will be borne with them, as the water itself reconstructs the field.

Let your body then be thought of as this field, and the flow of Life as the nectar of God from your heart. And may this field, then, release its dust particles—the old thoughts, ideas, concepts, and commands that you have given to it. Let each of your commands, in the manners in which you have controlled self, dissolve and melt into the flow of Life. And let them be carried forth in whatever manner that life would command within itself. And you will find your field being healed, and your body awakening.

There are many transformations the Spirit will bring to you, and this is why it is called the Holy Spirit. We are Æolus and Pallas Athena, of the ray of the Holy Spirit. That which dwells above all the Earthly conditions of life. We are of the eighth ray and dimension of life, which lies beyond the seven. The seven chakras are the seven rays that dwell within the current field of Earth life. Each of those rays must be awakened and enlivened. And they will be doing so one at a time, and yet all at once.

For a flow will begin in one, and as soon as it does so it begins in the other. And this flow downwards from Heaven—for it pours down upon the Earth—is God's grace and love returning to you. Even as a gentle rain pours forth from the clouds into the dry and parched soils of the Earth. And so this gentle rain will come as a raining cloud of *soma* and of light from above you. And there will be those times in the quickening process when you will accelerate your Being enough to feel the fountain of life rise up out of the spine and through the crown of the head. And you will feel the raining cloud of *soma* pour down around you. And you will sense its perceptions as it enfolds you.

Dear ones, this is the rain of Heaven that pours down around you. And you will feel it as much upon your skin, as in your body. And you will feel every organ enlivened with it. And as the rain pours forth, abundantly, it will pour forth in that sense canal that you call the spine. And there it originates itself into *amrita*, the liquid nature of God in the body. The liquid nature of God in the body is called *amrita* for it is that which brings knowledge, *rita*. And it is that which comes forth out of the central sun, the *am, amen*.

And I say to you then, dear ones, "This is the knowledge of life as it flows through the human body to the Spirit of Life in every cell. *Amrita* is the nectar in the spine that is physically and tangibly produced by the cells of your nervous system." This is a substance unknown to man at this time, but [which] has been greatly discussed by the ancients. And now, today, in this decade, *amrita* will become known and will be discovered as an element of life force, of life blood, of a more spiritual nature in the spinal column. It is not that which are called endorphins, or cerebral spinal fluid, for it is much more subtle than this. It has a life of its own, and its own hormonal balances. And this too will all be discovered as the raining cloud of virtue pours down upon you.

And, dear ones, out of this nectar shall come the awakening of all the senses, and their enlivening. The quickening through the third dimension will be altered. And one stream after another, one chamber after another, until all seven chambers of life perceptions are enlivened and awakened. And each chamber, and each sense perception, has a mind and heart of its own—has a throne and liquid light and dimension of its own. Beginning with the crown chakra it moves down through each of the chakras of the body, until all chakras are enlivened and awakened.

> And that which is its ultimate condition on
> Earth, the base of the spine, becomes
> filled with Life.
> And there it is, at the base of the spine, one
> discovers one's truth.
> One discovers the seed, the ancient tree.
> There it is [that] the nectar of the god and
> goddess within you resides.
> And there is it that your own Earth personality
> shall move forth out of its ancient seed
> and hiding place, into a new life of
> discovery.

And this discovery, dear ones, will take you through many journeys until once again you reach forth for Heaven. For what is above, is below, and what is below, is above. And that which is above rains down upon the Earth below until such time as the fields have been properly nourished. And then the seeds that have been planted therein will reach forth for the sun. And the rain clouds shall all move away, that the sunlight, and the liquid of light, [may] now nourish them.

Where once it was necessary for the Water of Life, for the *amrita*, now it becomes necessary for the *soma* of life, which is the light. And the light feeds the senses, as the sprout reaches forth towards the sun. It is the sunlight that now nourishes the new sprout. And it is [toward] this that the sprout reaches forth and spreads its branches. And so, dear ones, to rephrase for your understanding purposes we say to you, "Out of that which is a deep inner silence, and out of that which is the rising up of life within you towards greater freedom and success and releasing those controls and essences—then it is, that, out of the spine rises up a Light, a nectar, and creates a *quickening* within you. Until such time that it becomes like a fountain pouring forth out of the top of your head. My cup runneth over!"

And every cell of the body shall feel the raining cloud of *amrita*. And that raining cloud that pours itself into the spinal column rains down through the senses and through every chakra of the body, from the crown of the head down to the base, as though a liquid light pouring from cup to cup. Enlivening and awakening each of your sense perceptions with each of the chakras. From the crown through the third eye, to the throat, to the heart. From the heart to the solar plexus. And from the solar plexus down to the regenerative chakra which is called the second chakra. And down until it reaches the first chakra at the base of the spine. And there, as it affects the first chakra, a seed is formed, and that seed begins to sprout and reach towards the sun. The new awareness then begins to shine all around one, and the sense perceptions become one of Joy and of Light. And as that Joy and Light reaches out into Life, it is discovered that everything becomes fulfillment. The Light of the sun shines all around.

It is seeing then, that out of the nectar of your own

meditation, out of the joy of allowing yourself freedom, and the flow of life, the River of Life comes home. And as the river of life comes home, you have allowed yourself the freedom of perceiving. In this freedom of perceiving then, your seeds will sprout. And all things will come to you, and they shall be of perfection. And this perfection shall be of form, and light, and love, and the richest and the greatest of all things—God. God is the Central Sun. And this sun shall shine all around you. Everything that you perceive will be affected by it. You are in light now, you are enlightened now, and all that which you are shall be a living essence and being.

Each of these stages can be said to be an awakening. The first is the awakening out of that which has been control—the third dimension. The third dimension is characterized by control, and hardness, and density—weight, responsibility, and separation. All separation and duality form in the third dimension. Out of separation there is fear, there is pain, there is ignorance, the ability to ignore and turn one's head away from the truth. The ability to deceive oneself and to think other than what is. To perceive differences, and to understand the qualities of those differences as being important. To separate one from the other. These are all the sense perceptions of the third dimension, and they challenge one, they separate one, and they break one's heart. They break one's momentum of life, and they slow it down, for they are the brakes of life. And the acceleration of life then is curtailed, and the very motion of life to expand and to grow, is stopped.

And, thus, life proceeds into non-life, into non-sense perception, and into illusion. The illusion begins with sleep, and ends in death. And that illusion is perpetuated by mankind, again and again. But it is only an illusion, and not filled with truth. It will only perpetuate itself so long as each individual allows it to be so.

We say to you then, at this time, "That you can curtail that which is the motion of death, and reverse the aging process. You can in fact awaken the senses, no matter what stage you are on your journey." It can be said that those things that you are, can all be reversed. And that occurs by allowing the light to pour forth. First you must contact it, and this you will do in your meditations, even as we have guided you today.

But we would then say to you, and suggest to you, "The next [step] is to let it flow." And let the river of life grow from the center of your heart, and accelerate your Being. And you will feel the *quickening*, you will feel the tingling, you will feel the movement. And at times there will be dust particles that will be brought forth, brought to the surface. Things that you perhaps no longer desire, things that were thought to be useful when all of life was parched and dry, but now appear to merely muddy the condition of life as you are awakening to your sense perceptions. Allow those things to be washed free of you. That which is the river of life will do this freely for you. You need not even ask of it. It is part of its process, and its goal. *You need not even ask of it.* For it will remove these things from you automatically.

> And the third dimension perception then will
>   become less hardened.
> And will become more of Light.
> And you will feel brighter.
> And you will feel more free.
> And you will love yourself more freely.
> And you will contain yourself less frequently.
> You will restrain yourself less frequently.

And when the vehicle of life starts to move you will not step upon the brake, and brake it. You will no longer be bringing pain to yourself. But as the river of life flows through the sense canals, and through the dried and parched fields:

> Know there will be some breaking up of the
>   old soil.
> Know there to be change inevitable.
> Know the transformation of both your physi-
>   cal body and your environment, and all
>   of those things which you would see
>   will change, until such time as the flow
>   of Life is brought to peace and perfec-
>   tion—again.

The third dimension will begin to alter its form and its shape. It will be as though crystallizing into light. It will be as though its form becomes altered and reshapes itself. In this process then, you will have the discovery that your body is no longer tangible, but intangible. You will discover, through your sense perceptions inwardly, that you expand beyond the physical confines of the body. That indeed you are made of Light, of liquid Light. And of this liquid Light, that you are as far as the eye can see, and farther. You are beyond all sense perception. And this has brought the experience of Joy, and of one's own Condition, and of God in one, for you and God are the same and there is no difference between you.

All this shall occur as your third dimensional form moves to its next octave, to its next dimension of light. And as it does so, you will feel the raining cloud. And it shall come from above you. And shall pour down all around you. And this again will water the fields. And your sense perceptions will become of greater joy, and your body of greater transparency. And you will realize that all things are coming to you as *the Grace of God*. And they are being poured, blessing upon blessing, upon you. And there is no restraining them, for they are all a condition of Heaven poured upon the Earth.

And even when that pouring upon the Earth shall be as a rain cloud, and come as though in the night, with lightening and with storm. We say to you, "It is God's storm in you that is awakening, and that storm is a blessing of utmost love and attention." At that time be strong, and allow that which is forgiveness of self. And to be that which is part of the rain cloud pouring down God's love and abundance upon you, so that the fruit might be issued forth, and the seeds might sprout in the parched soils of the Earth.

And, dear ones, at this time we say to you, "This is the transition into the fourth dimension. For as the raining cloud pours upon the physical body in its form, you would know that *I AM* unlimited, *I AM* joy, and *I AM* this raining cloud of God Power. *I AM* that *I AM*. And all of this I shall become as my nature fulfills it, and my rain nourishes it." And so it is that you have the perception of two—the perception of yourself as divine, and unlimited. And yet the remaining soils of the Earth still formed, and [are] still ready for sprouting. And you will see how they are sprouting, and how they are growing.

The difference between the fourth dimension and the third dimension has much to deal with the perception. The perception of the divine in you becomes awakened in the fourth dimension where it is asleep in the third. And in the third, it is as though all is just of matter and separation, and everything matters, and everything is important, and bears conditions and responsibilities upon it. But that which is the fourth dimension is conditionless and free. It knows only its own inner motion. And that it knows to come from God, from its unlimited source. And as that Source pours forth from above one, it sees all life as a virtue. It sees nothing as destruction, but only as change. And sees transformation and healing, and the healing of the wounds for the gap.

The open holes are being closed.

> And, dear ones, as you recognize this trans-
> formation, you would see both the
> Heaven above and the Earth beneath.
> You would see the cloud pouring virtue of
> Life, and forgiveness into the Earth.
> And the circumstances and sequences of your
> life will change.

This is the opportunity that is being presented to every living Soul on Earth. And in this decade, all souls shall know the divine in them. This is the time of the second coming, it is the time of the Christ child to be borne. And that birth shall renew faith in God, and understanding in the unlimited condition that God has given to each Soul. And no Soul shall remain on the Earth without this experience. For those souls who would have this experience, it will be given to them. And for those that would not, they will be given an opportunity to dwell elsewhere. But for those Souls that remain with Earth, and continue with this Earth, they shall know God and shall know him as a Being of peace that dwells within. And through which all the rivers of life shall be sprouting and all of the conditions of life shall be had.

> For it is God's unlimited condition that flows
> through the human Soul.
> And it is God's unlimited Condition that has
> formed all of Life. And each of you then
> are in that Condition, and are a part of
> His sequence.

So allow yourself that freedom to flow with that sequence in the fourth dimension. Many of you are already entering into that phase. Most of you who would read this book have an understanding of the God within, and its precious power, and its forgiveness. And you would see the raining cloud as it pours down about you—transforming your physical body into light. The light body of that which you *are* exists in Heaven.

And at this time, in fourth dimension, you will perceive it as it exists in Heaven, and yet you will know yourself as possessing a physical form. This is fourth dimensional experience. And there are many qualities within it which shall grow in Light within you. Each of the chakras shall grow in light, and as they do so, until the final one is healed, which is your Earth chakra at the base of the spine, you shall be feeling partially of Heaven, and partially of Earth. And the conditions of Earth will yet be a part of you. As the soils of Earth are moved. And yet as those very soils of Earth are moved, they shall transform and heal into perfect godliness. And the Tree of Life shall sprout.

The Tree of Life is the fifth dimension, for it is this seed that reaches towards the light of the sun. It is this sense perception that begins to recognize all is divine. And the body itself is divine, and filled with light. And this light will grow, and it will expand, and you will feel the cells of your body literally tingling with Light. And as they reach out the light will grow even brighter. And as they perceive, each perception shall grow brighter. And all of Earth will be seen as Heaven. And there is no place to go, no place to exit to.

> Ascension *is not*, and *never is*, the leaving of
>   the Earth.
> It is the lifting of the Earth into Light.
> It is the perception that wherever one goes—
>   *all is God.*

And here, on Earth, Ascension must occur. For here on Earth the senses must be enlivened. And here on Earth they must perceive the nectar of the Central Sun of God. And that Light will be seen coming forth from every object of experience. From every object, and every form. It is this, then, that is the perception of the fifth dimension. Whereby the body has begun to perceive itself as Light, and that which is all around it as Light as well. And so all is seen as the divine vehicle of God, that it is God that is perceiving, It is God that is being perceived, It is God and every Earthly object and every sense perception. It is the Light of Heaven reaching forth for the sun. And here we have the essence of the fifth dimension, whereby in physical fact and physical form, as the Light of the senses becomes awakened to the realization that it is God, that the body itself becomes like God and filled with light. It literally will dissolve its Earthly appearance, and its form shall be a vehicle of Perfect Light and Ascension.

The fifth dimension then would be a body of light no longer perceivable by the third dimension. It will have reached beyond its own octave. The fourth dimension would still be perceivable by the third, for it yet has that quality of Earthliness even though the Soul within has been recognized to be of God's descent—descent into matter, and importance. We see then that the fifth dimension differs from the fourth, only in the sense of the senses. That the senses themselves begin to awaken their perceptual abilities. To know themselves to be God's Love and Light. And that this light has melting power, and that melting power is enriched with each perception. And as the senses reach forth for new perceptions, and new light and new love, the cells of the body begin to melt into that light and into that love. And all of Life is merged into One Light. This is the fifth dimension.

But beyond the fifth dimension, there is the sixth and the seventh, and more. And each of these are octaves of refinement. Of the quality and condition of life and existence. With each dissolving of a quality and condition, there is a reemerging with the eternal essence and oneness of life.

There are many octaves beyond the third. All of them are open to you. Each of your senses shall be opened in this way. For most of you it will take the senses of the Earth a full 2,000 years to return to the octaves of Pure Light and Pure Discovery.

But even now that Light is discovered within
you, and the fourth dimension is at hand.
You will live in a world of Perfection.
And you will know this Perfection to be God.

You will yet perceive It in form and reality,
however, and you will understand this
reality to be God's reality, with no friction.
There will be no human error.
There will be no human death.
There will be no human suffering, and no
human disease.

Once the transition has been completed into the
fourth dimension, and all of the dust particles have been
corrected and placed in their proper order by the flowing
river of life, that river of life will form itself into an absolute
perfection, which is friction free.   That *is* the fourth dimension—it is friction free.   Free of resistance and all
healing, for healing will have occurred, in perfection.

It's Earthliness, however, can be discovered to increase. And even from that place where there is no friction,
there can be seen the light and [the] rivers of life flowing.
And then one becomes exhilarated with the flow and freedom of God, and seeing God in all places. This then, will
create a sequence of time of about 2,000 years in which all
of Earth shall ascend into light. It shall transform of its own
velocity and its own nature, until it literally vibrates with the
quality and joy of God.

The exhilaration of God shall be so profound
as to melt all forms.
It is like a flame—that first is steady and

singular.

And as it begins to reach forth, it extends itself
to other flames.

And as those flames all gather together they
are seen as a blaze.

And they become excited in their blazing quality.

As life is seen with further and further oneness,
the fifth dimension shall unfold, and the
Earth shall ascend into Heaven.

Blessings to you ... I am Æolus, together with Pallas
Athena. We greet you with these understandings. They are
profound, and they are to be read many times. They will
awaken new parts and dimensions within you for they are
attuned in such manner as to create that dimensional frequency within you. And the sequence of events shall unfold
in perfection, even as they are given to you today. And they
shall challenge you from time to time. Melt with them and
release those challenges—as the water releases the dust
from the parched Earth.

And let that which thou art become known.
For that thou art—that *I AM*.
And we are One.

Blessings to you . . .

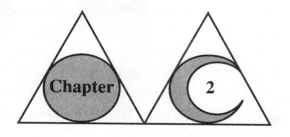

THE STAGES OF QUICKENING FROM THE 3RD TO THE 4TH AND 5TH DIMENSIONS

By Ascended Master Æolus and Lady Master Pallas Athena

It is with great Joy and great Love in our hearts that we greet you once again. And we bring forth this teaching of old—and yet of new. It is a teaching of the ancients, for it is the awakening of the ancient Soul. It is the awakening of the ancient gift of God to every human Being on Earth.

We are Æolus and Pallas Athena, divine complements, Fullness and Freedom. We bring to you, therefore, those things that are indeed the Gift of God and the Light of the Holy Spirit. For we are Masters of the Ray of the Holy Spirit, what you would call the White Light and the Freedom Flame. We bring forth to you then that which is perfect freedom, agility, and that which complements Heaven.

The subject of Ascension is a most interesting and exciting, and most delightful process for us to discover with you. For indeed, as *we* would see, you are ascended already! And that we know to be true. We would also recognize within you, the seat of the Soul in the heart, and how, even now, the Master sits upon the throne of the heart that you are, and welcomes your every wish and commands it to be so.

But in that which is the folly of human life and its experience, there is often a time when you do not know what you desire or what you request of this great and Holy Master, whose throne is in the heart. For in truth that which is your own heart does not understand life, for it is surrounded by many other authorities to which you have given your power.

And I say to you now, "Command that which is the Commander in Chief of all authorities and you shall know infinite and perfect peace." You shall know perfection even while on Earth. All of these things are at your disposal. They are timely—they would meet with you in good order and according to right time. All of these things that we speak about, dear ones, are the commands that you have given to all authorities on Earth. If that command be, "I am your servant," then you are the servant of those things that are here to serve you.

We welcome you with this understanding of perfect truth, for it is an understanding of life itself. The *I AM That I AM* is the Commander in Chief, not your human ego, or its perceptions, for your human ego and its perceptions are built from the very bonds that confine you. It is the limitation of self that you have learned to experience and to accept as life itself!

We are here to bring you perfect freedom from the bonds that charge you. We welcome this experience within you and accelerate it even now with the light of the Holy Ray of the Holy Spirit.

Let thy bonds be broken!
And let thy Soul ascend like a Silver Dove into
      Heaven!

I would ask that each of you now close your eyes and be filled with the Light of the Holy Spirit. May the very presence of God in your heart—the *I AM That I AM*—accelerate, blowing fast upon the Freedom Flame so that it no longer simply flickers and dies out, but grows strong and luminous within the spinal column and the entire body of your Being.

May all that which is already ascended be known! And I call forth that which is your own Being of Light, that Ascended Master bodily form that you already are, that you may know this form, that it may greet you, and that it may bring you mastery while on Earth!

Dearest ones, you who are Children of Light, you who are the great and mighty power of the Holy Spirit—you are the Ascended ones! I ask you now to come before these children— your chelas—to stand before them and to speak with them, and to greet them with open arms.

Each of you, my *chelas*, open your eyes now from within your heart, and you will see that Master that you are, there before you, luminous as a Holy Angel of God.

> Each of you are possessed of such a Soul as to
> achieve greatness.
> Each of you have that opportunity now laying
> before you to ascend.
> Each of you have a Holy Master to guide you
> that is your own *I AM Presence*.
> And there—luminous before you—He or She
> now stands!

I would have you to understand that this luminous Soul, this great Being of Light and this Master whom you have called is, indeed, a manifestation on a physicalized and dimensional level, an interdimensional level of perception, a concretized image of your own *I AM Presence*.

This Master form will take on the personality to whom you are most guided, to worship and to feel benevolence from, and compassion and wisdom. You may be experiencing this Master as something other than your *I AM Presence*, perhaps a presence that you have known or associated with another Master on Earth. Do not be confused by this, dear ones, for this loving form with which you are presented, in fact, actualizes a part of your own Being. Do not mistake appearances, dear ones, for these appearances are merely the projections of your own Soul, your *I AM Presence*! It will, in manifesting itself to you, take on whatever form you desire. It will bring to you acceptance and love and wisdom teachings in the form of whatever benevolent Master you require. For in point of fact, that Master is referenced by you as a result of your own love for Self, for that which is divine within you mirrors this great Soul of which you are reminded on Earth.

Each of you possesses such a memory as to go beyond your conscious mind. You will be drawn to certain circumstances and elevated states of consciousness that will remind you of that which you possess in your *I AM Presence* as Infinite Wisdom . . . Infinite Peace . . . Infinite Love!

Each of you, then, throughout your lifetime, will be drawn to circumstances and individuals and teachings— Masters far wiser than yourselves who are in truth only a part of yourself and reflect the perfect spirit of your inner Being, the *I AM Presence*.

We call on you to embrace this Holy Spirit that now stands before you, for it is your own *I AM*! It is your own divinity of Self! Embrace this form with this Master present and know it to be your guide and teacher, for you are the students, and your higher Selves are your Masters!

Put aside the form of human ego and its captive mind, and allow yourselves to embrace the infinite wisdom that your *I AM Presence* possesses. Bring forth out of Spirit those things that you are, and bring them forth through the teachings of the heart in the fond embrace of your favorite Master form that stands before you now!

Do you not feel an exhilaration and a *quickening*? This is the first stage of Ascension. For that which is the heart and core of life in the physical and material dimension of Earth begins to quicken, to lighten, to accelerate as a form of God is presented to it.

> Already the bonds that have ensnared you
>   have begun to be broken . . .
> What is the bond?
> What is its snare?
> It is the captive existence of human ego.
> It is the form that you willingly gave to this
>   Earth—and to Earth authority.

In so doing, you relinquished some of your own liveliness and life force. In so doing, that liveliness and life force began a process of decelerating, of slowing down its vibration, and condensates even as steam into water, and water into ice.

As this form becomes quickened, however, the process is reversed and you begin a return to your origin. The word "religion"—meaning bending back—is a teaching that brings all Souls back home. Home is where the heart is. And the heart is where God is. And a reminder of God brings a quickening to the heart.

As the heart accelerates, a communication is sent forth to every cell of the body. This communication is first registered by the brain and by the various organs of the body as a sensation of acceleration or quickening. Often you will feel such a quickening as just shiver or chill. Many of you have requested that your bodies give you signs when a truth is heard. You will find this manifesting in a number of ways, as what you call chicken skin or goose bumps, as what you would call a rush of Light, a flash of Light, a sensation or feeling of exhilaration. Though only for a moment, this, dear ones, is the Light that quickens—is the Light that liberates. It is the light that liberates from human form into divinity. It is the All Seeing Light and the Light of God that you all share.

Each of you on Earth possess such insight and power, for it was yours in the beginning, is now, and ever shall be yours. It is a world without end! The end is only the illusion of the human mind as it chooses one thing over another, turning its back upon the former and moving on. An end appears to have occurred. But there is no end in God, for all of those things that you *are* continue for lifetimes.

Even where you have turned your back upon them, they reappear. Life is endless, and all of those things which you once have manifested will return to you. They are all completing now. They are completing their cycles. The endless repetitions of human karma are all returning home. Their wheels are spinning homeward bound. And every Soul on Earth participates in this glorious and illustrious event!

In the next ten years of your Earth's future, all Souls on Earth will be guided home. Many Souls will choose to remain where they are for a while longer, they will be given an opportunity to do so. But the Earth vibration and planet itself shall remain homeward bound. Therefore those students of life who would wish to linger in the field of karma will be given an opportunity to share that life of karma with others not of Earth's origin. They shall be given this opportunity through a variety of means, to return to another dimension and to experience Earthly karma in that dimensional point of view.

But all of those Souls who wish to remain with Earth must understand that they are on a ship gliding through space whose time warp is now accelerating into the highest dimensional experience possible. It is for you to recognize and to understand that all of Earth is a planet in transition, and that all Souls associated with Earth are a part of that transition.

You cannot exclude any dimension of your own body from any experience that you would have, for every part of your body participates in that experience. Even so does every part of Earth participate in the Ascension Plan, whether they prefer it, whether they have chosen it consciously or not. All have chosen in spirit to return home one day—and that day has come! And this decade, is a day in the eye of God.

> All Souls are returning home!
> A great feast has been prepared for each one
> of you.
> A feast that was yours in the beginning, is
> now, and ever shall be yours as you
> come forth into your own Being.

Many teachers will greet you from both unseen planes and physical planes. They will express their knowledge to you—that knowledge which your own *I AM Presence* has requested.

Often you will not be ready for this knowledge. It is there simply to inform you and to prepare you. Each stage has its own receptivity, and the first stage is rejection—though it hears the words. And after that, the heart begins to quicken and to melt its boundaries and its confinements—its own limitations and authorities that it has placed around itself. As the very walls and armors of the heart begin to release and to melt down, the Ascended Flame will consume all illusions, and the brightness that shines forth will reveal only truth.

God has said that He will come to test the materials of your labors, and the Great Flame shall come forth out of Heaven and consume that which you have made. Those things that were made in Heaven shall last, and those things that were made of Earth shall be consumed, and then all that remains will be of God.

You will mourn under your labors and your losses, for in the beginning it will appear to you as though all is lost, but in the end all has been gained. That which once protected and armored you, now has been released, and the very Flame of God has been ignited. For what was once seen as a protection will later be seen as an armored wall that separates you from the very loved ones that you call in Heaven.

Blessings to you . . . I am Æolus [and] together with Pallas Athena, we greet you with a message of Ascension and information to teach you the Ascension Process. This has been the first phase of that teaching—to acknowledge your *I AM Self* and its presence—to have it embody a form before you that you might recognize *it* has a Master Teacher.

Perhaps in the beginning it is better for your will to understand this Master as separate from self but in the end, later with your development, you will learn to understand this Master as your Self with no separation between you. You will see your true form, the *I AM Presence* that you are, and the fullness that God gave to you in the beginning. As it is now, you labor under the burden of a physical body that is cumbersome by nature and carrying the weight of your ancestors of many generations.

All of your ancestors' authorities are borne by this body and accepted by the human ego that inhabits it. All of their forms of belief are embodied within the cells of this body, embedded in the DNA. On a very practical note, however, all of that which is called the cellular composition of the body is made of light, and, therefore, those beliefs are all illusion—changeable at any moment. But because they have been placed there a generation upon time, we see you, too, laboring under them and under their weight and strain. It is as though your mind were in a vise grip of attention, holding fast to the beliefs of your ancestors and to your society. Your human mind holds to these beliefs as if, were it to release them, it would surely die or perish, or some unseen force would come and take it away.

Dear Children of Light, we have a message of great importance for you to hear:

> There is no physical force in this universe,
>> save your own, that can take you away
>> without your willingness to go.

That is why we say there is no form in Earth or Heaven that can take you away. You are that God, and that God-presence dwells within you. Without *It* your very life force would be extinguished. For that very life force, infinitely small, is the power of God indeed!

It was your Christ that spoke to you with the words of faith. Faith the size of a grain of mustard that could move even a great mountain—that faith is the Flame of Life. Though it is infinitely small, and the mountain of your karma and its physical body seems infinitely large, even faith the size of a grain of mustard can move that mountain of karma.

It is the life force that is a part of you that can quicken. Many of you have seen a campfire that once existed and now exists only as an ember.

> One glowing ember is enough to remember
>   God.
> And to remember God is enough to fan the
>   ember to create the flame.
> One tiny flame is enough to ignite all of
>   Creation and create a bonfire of re-
>   joicing.
> Blessed ones, do not give up hope.
> Faith is your weapon against illusion.
> It is the only triumph, for it fans the Flame of
>   Life!

Your ego will try to confine that flame as it burns. It will build a wall around it, trying to protect itself and all that · it owns. But a flame once burning brightly must consume all things until only the flame remains. In the end, *all is God*, and all of those things which you would love would stand before Him. And, as you would see, all of those things do stand in His way. For were you yet to place your attention upon them, you would not have your attention upon Him.

This is understood only by the wise, for there are many who would make an illusion of Him and create false gods. These false gods do not necessarily have to be idolatry, formed in statues and the like. They are your very concepts and beliefs that form these statues in the first place. They can be as obvious and as simple as that which you call your leader, whom you worship and praise, or the dollar bill in your purse, or they can be as subtle as the very beliefs that you carry *about* God. Authorities come in many shapes and sizes, and all of which detract from the message of God to the human Soul.

I AM the Light . . . I AM the Way.

These were the words of your Christ. This Christ reminded you of that gift of Christ within you. The Christ within you is God in Motion. It is the living and awakened God. It is the living and awakened *I AM*.

As this flame of the I AM Presence starts to quicken, it grows luminously large and beautiful—it receives of compassion and grace. Grace is the outpouring or outflowing of God into human Life, into all avenues of life. It is the cup that runneth over. And even though it walks in the very shadows of death, in a field of illusion, and a world of forms and authorities, yet, the staff is strong and the wind will not bend it or break it.

As the Flame of Life becomes fanned, as the quickening accelerates, the human body responds—first with a shiver, and then with a sustained vibration of acceleration and quickening. Your breath and your heart will both quicken. The heart beating in [your] chest and the breath accelerating, you will feel as though a whirlwind of energy [is] within you, within the very breath that you breathe. And as that breath expands and continues to reach each cell of the body, the quickening continues, until a pulsation is felt throughout the entire physical form.

You will notice a mighty river growing in your spine, for this is the staff. It is the Staff of Life. It is the Tree of God. It is the *sephiroth,* and the *kundalini.* They are all the same. It is the quickening of this Tree of Life that will magnetize to it everything that it must consume. All illusions must become transparent until truth remains only!

As the quickening process accelerates, the Tree of Life, the Staff [of Life] becomes strong. You will feel the energy of Light within the spine connecting both heart and mind, soul and body together. It will move up, and it will move down the spine, until all parts of Self are recognized.

Wheresoever there is darkness within the human form, then the Light must penetrate there more carefully.

For these are areas of your own personality that you have hidden from your view. These are areas that you have chosen not to gaze upon, for they did not suit your reality upon the Earth. But this would be much like that which is the room of clutter that you hide from your neighbor's view. Perhaps it is an attic or basement, perhaps a closet in which you have chosen to hide the belongings that you wish for others not to view, including yourself.

These darkened places must be recognized, however, dear ones. They must become illuminated. And the first sight of them would bring you fear and would cause you concern. But on the path of the quickening, first there is acceleration and love, and then the flame becomes more dangerous and bold as it moves headlong into those experiences that you would not wish to share with others.

It is this challenge that we present to you in this Day of God—this decade. For [during] this time period you will be challenged by many forces of authority. And know, dear ones, these forces of authority are all self-made, and that they are all illusions created by your own Soul and its choices.

The *I AM Presence* is the Commander that would welcome all of your requests and honor them. Even where you would place greater authority elsewhere, it would give that gift to you. For *whatever* your desire, the *I AM Presence* must create. Where you give your authority to another, *It* must create it. Where you acknowledge that which is your own power, *It* also must create it. And where you acknowledge both, *It* also must create it. It will bring to you guiding Soul experiences of either challenge or benevolence, depending upon your persuasion.

The Soul is always being guided by your *I AM Presence*, even when it seems to you that it is not. It is a gift that comes to you from God. These experiences are meant to shake you and awaken you. They are meant to challenge and to shake out your fear.

> For where there is no fear in the heart, there is
>   no illusion.
> Where there is illusion, however, there shall
>   be fear.
> What do we mean by this?
> Fear is borne of illusion.

When you have created a false authority, one which you inevitably lose, you will innately be afraid of its loss. Those things which you fear, dear ones, are borne of your illusions, for you understand in your heart that you will lose them. The fear is the knowingness that you have placed your emphasis elsewhere than in God. Fear is the knowingness that you have placed your authority else-where than in God. It is to be said that all fear is borne [of] illusion. When you recreate truth in your hearts, by fanning the Freedom Flame, then you recreate the knowingness of God in your heart and there shall be no fear.

This trepidation is felt by every Soul on Earth. And as the body of light becomes cleansed of its darkness and illusion, its false gods and authorities, each Soul of Earth shall undergo a transformation.

Sometimes it is possible for the Soul to accept God all at once. In that great and triumphant moment, however, the quickening becomes almost insurmountable, impossible to control. It is as though it accelerates the very Soul out of the body, and one loses the experience of Earthly reality. This experience—which is called an "out of body experience" by most of you, by others it would be called "an acceleration into the Transcendent" where no physical form remains, only the Light of God—must be anchored and brought back. It must be brought into the Soul and into the physical form. In fact what has taken place is that your own awareness could not sustain itself in such Light and Power— it became lost. That awareness willingly and gratefully becomes lost in God. However, what was lost must be found again, and usually at the expense of losing God. And so the pendulum will swing from such God experiences to human reality. You will feel in one moment exhilarated, and the next confined. You will feel the freedom taken away from you, only to be remembered and to be praised. But, dear ones, the pendulum will swing again and again.

Our caution and our recommendation is for each one of you to be "aware" throughout all of the quickening motion of your physical form, its body and its awareness, its heart and soul. [And] as the quickening process accelerates within you, that you not leave this body behind, but take it with you.

This is the definition of Ascension—that you are not to leave behind those things which you have made, but you should create them now with Heaven's tools. This means that that which has become physical and condensed will now melt down and transform. The very material and substance of the human body will be caused to be made of light.

As Jesus accomplished this task, an image was created on the cloth that surrounded his body. The electromagnetic chemicalization that took place in his physical form was so immense and spectacular in that moment that it left an image in the shroud. Today it is well known that such a shroud exists. Whether it is the shroud that you possess already or another, does not matter. The truth has become illuminated, that that which was Jesus' shroud does exist, and its power—the power that it holds from the transformation of Ascension of this one Being of Light—is an inspiration for all to behold.

Each one of you will undergo a similar process, perhaps not in the three day time period that it took Jesus to create his Ascension, but it shall be over a longer period of time that your bodies will ascend. They have already begun this process with each quickening. Each quickening shifts the awareness and attunes the cells. Each DNA structure becomes altered when a current of light passes through it.

The illusions of before shall be overcome as the sun grows brighter. A false god can only be seen as truth when the light is dim. But when it is that the sun glows brightly, you recognize each Soul on Earth as a Soul like your own. No greater—no less than. All equal in the eyes of God. And whatsoever authorities they have given to you—you have given to them. They are entrusted with that gift, but they are no better, or worse than yourself.

We would have you to understand then, with this realization, that they cannot serve you ultimately in finding the Kingdom of God or creating His Kingdom on Earth. Only you can do this, for only your Soul has the power of the *I AM*. That *I AM Presence* is present for your self and your self alone. And were you to be one of those compassionate Souls to give gifts to others of healing, we say to you, "Call upon their *I AM Presence* to acknowledge this healing, for as each of you have recognized, you cannot heal another unless they are willing to heal themselves." In truth, no Soul on Earth heals another save God within them.

Blessings to you then, dearest ones, for we have begun now the second phase [of] instruction. That which is the reconstruction of physical form out of the quickening process. This, too, has many stages. One, the illumination lasts longer, and in that process a quickening continues to release and to shake free the illusions that bind. The confinements of the human ego and their authorities are to melt away as one begins to perceive them for what they are, merely separations of inanimate matter. We see that [inanimateness of thought form] becoming more animate with the light and power of your own *I AM Presence*. We see the garment wrapped around the Soul now being unraveled, as the light and power of the mighty *I AM Presence* becomes illuminated.

The DNA was condensed, dear ones, about the Soul. It was lifted and transformed by the very illusions that you carry in your human ego. What was once simply *thought* has now become matter, the material of the universe of form.

How was that form created? How was thought crystallized into form? The generations of your ancestors, created over time that [form] which you know as genetics. The power of their thought did it. It was the authority created in them, strong enough to create the threads of reality known to you as genes.

> These genes yet carry the thoughts and feelings of your ancestors.
> And as they begin to melt from the heat of the quickenings, they will appear one by one to your view.
> Even as they did to those who came before you.

The closets of the DNA are open now and all transformations include the gene pool, or shall we say, the melting of old authorities carried by them. It is this melting process, the coming alive of the inanimate—encrusted thought forms—that shall liberate the Soul from its hiding place.

This begins then a new phase and a new quickening, for the embodiments of old will now be liberated. No form will remain the same. You have traveled through time on a spiral staircase, traveling downwards into the third dimension of reality. With each step you lowered your vibration, condensed of your form, and limited of the very essence of your power. You wrapped the cloth of belief about yourself and called it home, encasing your Soul forever. You knew each of your ancestors in advance, and saw them coming. You embraced them, and called them home or family. You wrapped their clothes about you, and forgot of your essence and your name.

Now you live in a masked identity, covered by the travels of your ancestors, imprisoned by the controls they bestowed on you. Where once you lived with infinity and with God, now you live with limitation and death. Your illusions lasting only a hundred years or more. Your bodies have become statues of living memories re-enacting the experiences of your past.

Soon you will be completing this journey and be called home. There you will be perfect again with the Father/Mother of All Creation. You will live in the Garden of Beauty where your form will last forever in the Light.

You are on this journey now, and remembering where you have been. The records of the past have not been known to you until now. The veils have all been lifted, and the knowledge of the journey of humankind has been opened to you. It tells you of your future, even as it describes where you have been in your past. The journey of Atlantis and Lemuria will all be open to you—the memory of things long forgotten. Four and a half million years of physical descending from light into matter is involved. Your cells remember this process and now return.

Liberate yourselves (your cells) from these experiences now as we take you on a journey back towards your link with Heaven. Liberate your heart and mind from the grip of Earthly power, so that the realignment and reconstruction of the physical form may begin. We ask you to receive this now, as we begin a visualization and meditation to this extent.

We ask you simply to stretch and breathe. And as you stretch and breathe feel the light pulsate through you. With this you begin to know the motion of God and its power. This is as it was in the beginning, even as you were with Him. This motion of God, and its Power, is Supreme. It is functional. And it Liberates.

As the motion of God continues to reach your extremities, every cell becomes consumed in this flame. Each cell becomes reprogrammed and readjusted to higher frequencies of light and understanding and perception.

Each cell becomes attuned to whatever qu light will pass through it. Your cells have all been modified, and will be modified many times more, depending upon the current and frequency of your vision and life force.

Each of you will determine this for yourself. Thus far, as a planet you have determined to create a third dimension. The third dimensional point of view is one of limitation and death, a limitation to your human freedom, and a condensation into physical reality.

This condensation into physical reality has had certain appropriate measurements, [which are] determinable by your limited science. But as the frequencies of life become more accelerated and quickened, the very physical cells will begin to reorganize and re-pattern of themselves. Your chromosomes and DNA will all begin to be altered. There will be no memory of a past. There will only be its illusion. That which will be the illusion shall be a transparent form, like a narrow shell.

To experience this we ask you now to bring forth, to call forth, the Infinite Light. With your eyes closed for a moment, call forth the Infinite Light from your *I AM Soul or Presence* within you.

Now ask that your Master Consciousness step inside of you and embody that which is your physical form. As it does so, feel the quickening and the acceleration, the dimensional shift in your perception as it goes beyond your limits.

Allow the Light to spread and to shine clear of any resistance. Release those resistances now! Let them go as the Light will pass through them. Light has the infinite capacity to travel anywhere It likes. There is no physical form that can restrict Light. In some measure, in some way, a photon will pass through even the most solid object. So it is that as your own awareness stretches, [and] you will stretch beyond your limitations into that which is the Infinite Light.

Let the Infinite Light grow strong and let that which is its universal application be known by you. As the light [of your] *I AM* [*Presence*] shines within you, the Infinite God shines with you. The light that you are, is the Light of God. The Light of God has always shone within your own life force. You are a part of God. *You are a cell in the Infinite Being*.

As you acknowledge your own infinitude, you acknowledge that you are infinitely present and wise. All time is within your hand. To grasp this is to understand Infinite Wisdom and Potential. It is to rest in the Heart of God, which is the seat of your own heart.

Recognize now, that as the Light shines brightly, it seems to overtake and stretch beyond the form that you identified as self. You begin to see that your own form is but a chalice to hold the nectar of God. You begin to understand that you are this Light, and that the chalice is but the container.

This is the first recognition of the dimension of perception called the fourth dimension. For here it is that your own confusion about the nature of life is finally dissolved and you recognize that you are Light, and Light is your true form.

You yet perceive the chalice, however, and know it to be real. But from your own dimensional point of view as you enter into the fourth dimension, it is as though the third dimension only holds or houses that which is the light. The Light *is* who you are.

Who is the chalice, and how is it formed? It was formed and possessed of all the authorities that you have given to it. For each request that you have given to your mighty *I AM Presence*, the Commander in Chief, [it] would create a form for you. And with each form that was created, another brick was added to the structure of the physical body.

The physical body itself is a structure like any building, created out of your thoughts. And as each thought is mounted upon the other, it creates a physical form for you to inhabit. It will protect you against whatever elements you have chosen to dwell in. It will choose wisely those things that you would need in advance. Your own physical forms will adapt to weather conditions and to personality conditions. All of the systems that you will engage in, your personality self will create, and bricks will be added to the body to protect you.

This is the chalice that you have formed. It can also be known as a chariot for the Light of the Soul. And when it is that the chariot can no longer sustain the abuses of physical life and becomes broken down, it is discarded for another. But the Soul itself is eternal. It was given that gift by God.

Now as a fourth dimensional being or a being entering the fourth dimension, you begin to understand that *you* are this Infinite Light and its infinite potential, and you yet have a chalice in which to perform.

We say to you now, "View this chalice with even more Light!" And you begin to see that it is not solid but composed only of thoughts and perceptions. It becomes transparent, as though paper thin. Even as you witness it, you see that you are beyond your own condition.

This is a more accelerated form of the fourth dimension, for in its higher stages the chalice itself becomes more transparent so that it is just barely visible to your eyes. In this way, however, you will learn to accept that you are the infinite God and that the mighty *I AM Presence* is your gift.

We say to you, each of you have a task to perform on behalf of God. For every cell in God's body has His infinity and His infinite purpose. All cells will spontaneously cooperate with one another as they become realigned with the truth of God in them, for they are all one motion.

Were you to be physically embodied in anything other than the image of God, we would see the cells of your body all traveling in different directions and you would not survive. You would literally fall apart in a million pieces! And no life force would be remaining to hold you together.

> But the Life Force that holds you together is
>> named—Love.
> And Love is the grace and goodness of God
>> that unites all things.
> Even were they to begin to separate, Love
>> would bring them back.
> Love is the charm of Life!

In the first phases of Ascension we discussed the importance of Faith. Now we must discuss the importance of Love. Love is the power by which all this universe is held together.

First, out of that Faith came the power of the quickening, and that quickening's flame began to express itself as existence. Out of that then, there was what can be seen as Hope. For from that which is called the Power, Hope emerges. Hope that is the presence of God. Hope—that is the perception that the light passes beyond its own condition. Hope that the light will eventually triumph and its power become infinite. Hope that the quickening process will create Ascension, and eternal life will be given to you, even in physical form. Hope that all that that you are will become one with God again. And this, then, becomes Love!

Love is the choice that creates the fifth dimension when all things become united!

While you are yet in the fourth dimension, however, we would have you to perceive form outside the body. There you will recognize the chalice still holds the Light. And you will see that even though the chalice has become transparent to your vision, it yet is solid to another's. You will recognize that even as you pass through life knowing who you are as the Infinite God, yet others will perceive you as an individual, and will understand your ways as they would see them. Therefore they would not always know of your wisdom, for their eyes cannot perceive *you*. They only perceive the chalice!

This is a perception of the fourth dimension: In the first phase of Ascension, which is to take place in this decade, all Souls of Light will recognize themselves as Light. Their chalice will begin to transform and the electromagnetic patterns realign. All things will become synchronized with God once again, and all the infinite patterns of the universe will be explored. The vision, however, of the chalice will remain somewhat the same.

You will not yet ascend into full light in the way in

which you might imagine—as all of Earth dissolving and being physical no more. No, you will yet have a physical existence, but it will be fourth dimensional existence, one in which the duality of life is shared, in which all of Light becomes known to you, and all of physical existence shares knowingly in that Light and becomes modified.

The modification and reconstruction process of your planet Earth will begin in the later portion of this decade, as all of the systems of the Earth become realigned to truth. This is also part of the physical Ascension that must take place in this Day of God [this decade].

In the first portion of the Day, it is as though the Soul awakens and sees the Light dawning. But as the dawn gets brighter and brighter, and the full noon now becomes explored, all the things that were hidden will be revealed. By 1995 or 1996 of your years counting, there shall be such explorations of hidden things, that nothing will remain unexposed. In that time period then the Light must shine in such a way as to recompute the systems of the Earth, to reformulate them, to reconstitute them to be in harmony with the infinite God and the infinite wisdom of the universe. The Light must flow one to the other, and flow harmoniously without friction. All of your sciences will embrace a science of friction free superfluid conductivity—all things in harmony with each other.

In addition to this, your own physical forms shall be transformed and re-embodied. They will be re-embodied with spirit, with the spiritual essence and dimensions of who you are. This will be the completion of third dimensional transition into the fourth dimension of Ascension.

As for the physical reconstituting of the body into complete Light, this will take approximately another two thousand years. So it shall be that as the third dimension took two thousand years to complete of itself—once it had determined to do so with the birth of Jesus on Earth—now it will do so again with the rebirth of the Christ in every Soul, for the fourth dimension is the Second Coming. It is the coming of the Christ Child within each chalice. It is the Light of the Living God overflowing the chalice even in the shadow of death, until all that which is death is seen as an illusion, a transparent reality which once held lordship over the Soul because the Soul's authority was given to it. Now the Soul must reclaim its own authority and that Ascension process reconstituted and begun.

I welcome you now into that which is the agency of Love. Sit back and breathe once more the Light that you are, the light beyond the chalice, the light of the Holy Spirit, the Holy God Presence *I AM*.

And out of the *I AM* comes Love. This Love would join together with all things. As it joins together, visualize those things that you love one by one being embraced by you. As they are embraced by you and the Light, they become more than the chalice, they become the Light Itself. Indeed, all of those things that you would love so dearly, would melt and be consumed by the Light [of your mighty] *I AM*.

This Light of the God *I AM*, the God Presence, and the Inner Christ will embrace everything until all things become a part of you, a part of God *I AM* once again. All of life will become consumed in this way.

Embrace them all one by one.
That one that you Love so dearly, bring he or
she into your heart until they, too, become
one Light.

Those children and those gifts that are around you, bring them in to that Light until they, too, become One.

Those parents and friends, bring them in one by one in order of love appearance, before you, until they, too, become One.

Those things on which you sit, those things for which your body has been endowed, those things that surround you in the room, in the house, bring them in until they, too, become One.

All Light sustains everything in the universe.
And all things in the universe are all Light.
Bring now the clouds of illusion of your past
into the Light, and it becomes One.

Bring now the surrounding atmosphere, the houses, the buildings, the forms of human lives, the automobiles, and all the machineries of life, bring them in. Your entire city brought into the heart and into the Light, and it, too, becomes One.

Bring now your troubled nation and its perspective of the world into your heart, into the Light, and it, too, becomes Light. See all the troubles and concerns of your national heritage being brought into the Light, so that the tremors that they have created on your human forms might be dissolved with Love. This is Infinite Love, my friends, this is Infinite Love! Bring them all into this Love and they become one with Light.

Bring now your unhealthy Earth into this Light, so that all of those things that are of Nature are brought into the Love. They will be infinitely responsive and rejoice. You will see them become excited and a quickening take place. The Earth shall quicken itself into completion and into perfection, and all the environmental ills shall be healed, as though over night. Bring them into the Light and they become One.

And all the national boundaries now, bring into your Light that they might become One.

One Earth,
One Perception,
One Love of God.

Bring the entire Earth now and Her body with all of its people and all of its beliefs, all of its Heavens and all of its astral worlds into the Light, and it, too, becomes One with the Light.

And bring now all of Earth's brothers and sisters, who are waiting for you in Heaven, for all of the planets of this solar system have all ascended and are waiting for you in the fourth dimension. Bring them in, until they, too, become One and you are reunited in peace and brotherhood.

Now we see the path and course of time, that in the next two thousand year sequence not only will Earth become Light, but all this solar system will ascend into the Pure Light. There will be no physical universe, as you understand it, to your perception in two thousand years. It will be all *One.*

It will be a light world freed of any density, any limitation. All of life shall be the infinite life and the infinite joy of God! It will be sustained through the current of Love that joins all things together and it shall be growing by the grace of God, which is the momentum of God's desire through the *I AM Presence* in every heart.

Blessings to you! These experiences represent to you the transition from third dimension to fourth dimension in this Day of God (this decade), and the two thousand year sequence to the fifth dimension.

The final phase of fifth dimension is the operation of all things as Light. The entire solar system will join with that which is the Light of its True Form. There will be no physical solar system as you recognize it in two thousand years, it shall return to its full velocity as Light.

Each Soul on Earth and all the systems of planets will have accepted that condition as their own. They will re-embrace that which is their God-maker. All things will return to their origin. Life will yet continue, but on a lighter plane, for indeed, there are many dimensions to human life, the third dimension being but one of them, and that being the most crude.

You are now ready, dear ones, to ascend into the fourth dimension in this Day of God. Then Godspeed! May the quickening accelerate within you, and may the Light of God shine all around you! May the chalice of God's vehicle be known by you! And may you know yourselves to be Light!

I am Æolus together with Pallas Athena, and we welcome you with this vision of Ascension. A vision of Ascension that brings to you the most completeness and perfection that you have ever known or cherished. Let go of those things which confine you now and trust in the motion of God. That once that flame has been ignited, it shall consume all things in its path until no illusion remains, only Light!

Blessings to you! The Quest of the Light is to consume all. These are the Teachings of God. I AM the Lord thy God, thou shalt have no other gods before ME. I AM the God I AM. I AM That I AM. And all of Life is before ME.

Blessings to you . . .

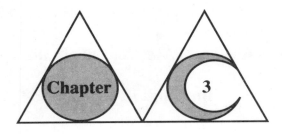

By Ascended Lady Master Kwan Yin, and Masters Ezekiel and the Merlin

KWAN YIN:

The Soul, which has been captivated by its own beliefs from generation to generation, is now breaking out of its shell like a rose blossoming out of an old bud. We ask that you recognize the emergence of an entirely different vibrational Being into a physical condition that has heretofore not supported that vibrational activity. Much that you would understand as physiological will move in a new modality of vibration, accelerating beyond human consciousness perception. It will accelerate into an entirely new vibrational plane of existence.

Heretofore all medical science has judged and understood the human condition in terms of its own mortality. There is very little of this understanding that will be useful in the future, however, for it is all part of a mortal and failing condition. We are now moving into that which is termed "unlimited science," where medical science would be utilizing the field of superfluidity rather than the field of normal conductivity on Earth.

As you are recognizing then, a whole new velocity of being is emerging in the cellular material. The old cell itself carrying the beliefs of its ancestors which limit this new activity. Each of those limitations would be seen first as thought forms that exist or co-exist with the DNA. These limitations [thought forms] are on a substance level similar to the amino acids, but more subtle than the amino acids. They have yet to be discovered as cellular material. These thought forms are composed of compacted thoughts and ideologies that have formed into a crystalline structure that exists or co-exists with the DNA. They have caked themselves about the DNA and veiled it over. They have, indeed, influenced the very structure of the DNA, such as to bring forth certain personality traits as well as biological traits over time.

The substances of these old thought forms are now *being released* from the cellular material and from the genetic code. They are beginning to influence the structure of the blood as well as all of the structures of human physiology. The conduction of all electrical currents in the body are beginning to alter as the very structure of the body is altering. Layer by layer these elements are being released from the physical system of all beings.

Even those walking a normal course of events, are being influenced by a radiation of light of such magnitude as to bring forth the emerging Soul. It is possible now, in this time period, to bring back this emerging Soul or revitalize this emerging Soul into its true essence in a physical condition. This physical condition in itself will transform as the Soul's radiation contacts it, for the Soul's radiation is unlimited, whereas the physical condition is limited.

All of this, you understand, is now to radiate its own unlimited condition through this limited physiology and bring it up to a level of transparent existence where it is luminosity and not just physicalness. *Luminosity means it radiates from within itself.* It requires no source of outside influence for nutrition. It requires only itself and its guiding light.

As this light is now being guided into the body, the body doesn't always know which way to turn. It is often confused because its old programming has told it [that] it is a limited condition based upon certain tenets of survival. It is confused when it is informed that it no longer requires those old tenets of survival, that it is now new physiology emerging, and that that physiology is self-sustaining by its own influence of light and power. The gifts of the Soul are many to the physical existence, but the organism of physical truth does not accept those unlimited conditions. It persists in holding on to its own mortality. Therefore there is a struggle. It is as though a tug of war is taking place back and forth between the two beliefs. There is an alternating of current that yet persists within physical existence.

By one, such as yourself, coming into contact with a Soul of higher power in nature [such as your client, or peer], you may call forth that higher power and stabilize it into a physical condition. And then you can call forth those elements that contain within the DNA the truth, and they will respond to you as though they were living beings. We ask you to consider the DNA and understand it as being merely a reflection of the Soul, recognizing that at the very core of the DNA is a living being that looks much like yourself, in that it is a being of light, of human form.

This human form would be the personality deva of the DNA.
The personality deva is in every way identical to the absolute Soul that is emerging.
It contains as its proper and full Essence, all Light and Power, and all Knowledge and capacity of the Soul.

Wheresoever this personality deva is located in the physical body, it has also a given task assigned to it. And that given task is associated with the muscle tissue or with the bone or whatever it is that it is now functioning under. It is therefore creating limitation within the unlimited. But that unlimited capacity will now start to function as a universal balance and create within the cellular material a new organization based on truth.

As you call forth the emerging Soul, recognize that what you are truly calling forth is the unlimited knowledge of the Soul. It is beyond all of that which is considered as its DNA program, for the DNA program is like an old skin that is being shed. And as that old skin is being shed, you would see emerging forth a new and more vital being.

The DNA is releasing its own encodings, which have been passed down from generation to generation, and will no longer be passed down. The very electromagnetic current that has held it in place is altering and will no longer hold it in place. It will be released through the blood stream and out of the body.

As it is released through the blood stream it will cause many confusing elements to come to the surface. Those things that will be seen as illness and congestion, they will not be understood, for many will not be able to be diagnosed. They have not been seen in human history. Or perhaps for a moment, those elements from past plagues, generations ago, will suddenly come to the surface to be healed and cleansed all at once.

And one will have the appearance of an illness when in truth it is merely emerging from the cellular material and being released from the body.

All of this, too, you understand. But what is not so easily understood, is that the perfection underneath it all, guiding the intelligence of every cell, is a personality that is similar to the Soul itself. This personality might be called upon as a living being and spoken to. The cells will guide you, as you can guide the cells. The most important thing to remember here, is that:

The cell is a living intelligence full of Love.

It has been abused and it has been pushed into the background. It has been hidden from view. It has felt as though misused and unloved.

As you call on this personality then, call forth the living essence of the Soul first. You must call forth this ultimate vitality first, so that there within physical form, there is emerging a new life force. So that when the cellular material is called forth, these angels, these devas of intelligence will now recognize that here in physical form is their counterpart in truth. And they will be accepted.

If you would not call forth that living Soul first, these devas would then respond and find themselves in a vacant body. A body that has lost its vitality and will again replace truth with its own beliefs.

And so first one must call forth the living Soul, next one calls forth the living Soul in the DNA, and the two then begin to cooperate together.

You would ask instructions of the DNA, and they would give to you their own personal idea forms of what steps can be taken. These idea forms will be born out of truth as they are filtered through the physical condition of that physiology. They will speak to you in their own ways.

They will speak to you of *moment* and not of *future.* The moment will be precisely what is required by the Soul and its physical condition to change into its future.

In each moment, then, you will unfold truth. Do not be surprised that each moment does not follow in a natural and logical sequence.

For in many cases, where the Soul is more accelerated than the physical condition, it will have to modify itself more rapidly than the human mind can comprehend. And it will not appear to be logical, simply because not all the steps are seen as obvious. In truth, they are all very logical and sequential. But many things cannot be observed by the human eye.

And so we would say to you, "This is the greatest challenge of your life for it is a challenge of faith. Faith in that which is *truth*, beyond that which is *understanding*." For in understanding there is limitation. And wheresoever there is limitation, one must bridge the limitation to the unlimited by faith.

> *Much of your work in the future will involve deep faith. Indeed, the energy and power of the Soul will be blossoming through you, so strongly that it will associate itself first as light and only later as knowledge. You will see, of course, the two almost coinciding as they come forth, but there will be many times when you know not what you do until you have done it.*

You will have to recognize in each stage that new teachings must emerge. You will not confine yourself to the old. But rather allow yourself or permit yourself to take great and bold steps into new arenas. Even challenging your own basic tenets of belief in order to provide that which is necessary for the individuals who have come for your service.

Dear one, you are a master in disguise. You are a master in that which is termed the physical. You are a master of light who carries great wisdom and understanding. You are on an equal plane with ourselves, though you are indeed in physical form and therefore have to exist under the veils of physical understanding. We say to you in truth, "You possess all knowledge that we possess. And therefore you have the capacity to draw forth that knowledge at any one moment. It only requires an opening that is provided to you by those who come to you."

> You cannot provide to this Earth what it does
>   not require.
> That is the only Condition under which you
>   live.
> All else can be given.

And indeed you will often find yourself giving more than what the moment requires, for you give to it [that of] its next step or next phase. You will soon be advancing to such a degree as you will have to follow that which is your inner heart and guidance at all times. It will not be in a logical sequence. It will often appear to you as though it has no roots.

It is as though you were to become more and more a citizen of Heaven, rather than a citizen of Earth. And the work that you will do will be as one who is administering to the citizens of Earth. You will begin to see them more and more as physical Beings and yourself as light. You will see the direction into which they are moving and you will understand yourself more as a ministering angel coming to this Earth to serve them.

As it is today you yet associate yourself much with them [these citizens of Earth]. You see them in a condition similar to yourself. But we would have you more and more to understand that you are to accept that light and to radiate it. In all humility and all faith, you are to radiate that which you are. You are to serve others as a guiding light. And not just simply as one who is teacher, not just one who is healer, not just one who carries knowledge and information and instruction. But rather, one who is *light*.

First and foremost, that is who you are. And the service that you provide is more subtle and more powerful than any other service that you could provide otherwise. There is no such thing as any finite knowledge on Earth that can serve this planet at this time. For indeed, all finite knowledge is becoming infinite knowledge. And therefore it will stretch beyond its own boundaries into that which unlimited truth. Unlimited truth as a priority experience implies that unlimited truth cannot be confined into formulas. It is rather digested by that which is termed a human condition and utilized in each moment, moment by moment by moment.

I AM Kwan Yin. I am the guiding teacher of all healers on Earth at this time. I AM bringing forth a new radiation of healing. And all those who are awakened to this

...aling will be serving a new vibration of being. We will say to you in truth that that which I once brought to this planet is now no longer to survive in its old form. For I was the founder of what you will call acupuncture. But this is an understanding of Earthly meridians and etheric forms that are no longer applicable to the human condition. And were one to organize life around those old principles, they would indeed be reinforcing a prison out of which the Soul is now trying to emerge. The principles of acupuncture, the principles of all ancient science, including vatic science, all of these things now are indeed only reinforcing an old prison of physical condition that is no longer to survive.

We are bringing through a new radiation at this time, carried by the Emerald Flame and by the Magenta Flame. The Magenta Flame is the next flame of the heart. It is the next awakening of the heart. As you bring forth your work, you will use the healing flame of Emerald, and you will use that through your own physical condition. As you do so, you will radiate an energy vibration that will create a sequence of events, both for yourself, your environment, and all those who are in the environment, whether it be one individual, two, or many. The sequence of events will be as follows: First, as the radiation is emitted, you will lift the very quality of the molecular condition of your atmosphere. The atmosphere will continue to hold form, but will become more transparent. From your own vision point of view you will seem to feel as though you have entered into a new dimension of experience. The physicalness of all objectivity will become more and more transparent until literally you can see through it.

The Light radiation, therefore, that you are emitting has created an Ascension process. This Ascension process will enable the doors of the physical body to open. If they would have remained on another dimension, the Soul that you are now requesting to come in would not find an open door and be permitted to come. Instead, you will emit a vibration of truth. This vibration of truth prepares the physical condition by lifting it.

As it enters into its new accelerated state, the Soul itself in all of its purity and truth, not that which has gone through transmigration, but rather that which has undergone only truth comes forth. This is the electric current of the Soul, the true Soul and the true velocity created by God. This Soul has been undisclosed on the Earth vibration, and is now coming to the Earth vibration for Ascension.

As those doors are opened, the Soul enters in. And as it enters in, you call it forth and speak to it, rather than to the physical beings. It is as though you will look out over that individual or over that group of beings and you will literally see or imagine seeing their Souls. Then you begin to speak to that community of Souls, rather than to a community of individuals. You attune to their vibration and to their needs and to their truths. As you speak the words that come forth, they may not be recognized as those that you would use.

You would speak to those *Souls*, therefore, first and

foremost. As you do so, it is the physical ears which are listening to you, and even while they are straining to understand you, the very Soul itself is being called forth into the body. For by the body trying to understand what is spoken to the Soul, [it] then seeks out the Soul and accepts it. And the Soul then enters into a physical condition whereby before it was only permitted to stand by the wayside.

Once the Soul has entered into the body, the rest is automatic. Cell by cell, the body can begin to transform with or without your knowledge and assistance. The primary work has already been done. The rest is fine tuning. All of the sacred devices that you will come upon will all be placed in your possession for a reason. But they are not to be strictly used. You must be innovative with them. You must challenge the very velocity out of which they were made. You must increase their frequencies always. For all of that which carries electromagnetic current must be increased in its velocity. You will do so by your own living consciousness.

You will notice on many occasions you will get different readings than others will. Primarily because of the influence which you radiate even into the electrical equipment. Electricity is a current of light. It is a current of *Life Force*. It does not matter what its form, it carries that which is Life Force always. So as you would radiate your own Life Force, you would lift the Life Force of the electric current and transform it into the highest needs possible on Earth.

You will bring forth that which is your true radiation of Spirit. For this then, you, too, must always be clear and be in your own perfection as it exists in Heaven. For this then we have our suggestion. Look for that Master, or Masters, that you have admired while here on Earth, and know them to be a reflection of your true radiation of Spirit in Heaven. Meditate upon them and the vibration of power and Life Force that they represent to you. Know that as you do so, you are, in fact, energizing your consciousness on Earth with that power. And that power is your Self, as you are in Heaven. Each moment that you receive this Power, it will energize you and fill your being. Then you can become that Being on Earth and fulfill your mission.

Blessings to you ... *I AM* Kwan Yin, the Lady Master of all healing on Earth, and keeper of the Emerald Flame.

EZEKIEL:

I send a blazing light before you! And I call you forth, for I AM present, and I ask you now to reach out with your right hand, as though reaching out for that which is the light. That you might hold it fast and say, "I AM." And as you would experience of this mighty power, know that I AM with you, I AM Ezekiel. And I come to you therefore on high with all my light and my spinning wheels of fire. And I create that for you, that is a blazing path before you. It is only required of you to reach out for it and to proclaim, I AM. For such as your greatness proclaims, for the God that has made you is indeed within you now.

And all that which lays before you is as a parting of the ways of your earth's reality, into the blazing light of truth of its future. But this truth is not yet perceivable by the norm. Indeed even those of you who cast your garments forth and now are emerging naked into Heaven, we say to you, even now as you step forth, even you cannot see all that there is to know. But so be it. For such is the way of truth.

We cannot have you go where others will not go. We can only have you to go in those places where they, too, are willing to go, for they must follow you, and they must honor you. And they must be tempted in all Earthly ways possible to emerge from the shadow of their own reality into the light of truth of the new. And so we shall come blazing from Heaven with spinning wheels of fire. And yet I say to you with all the spinning of truth, there shall be that which is present and that which remains the same as the *I AM Presence* dawns within you.

You must know that which is your power and your fire, and you must honor it always. You are that which stands in the light of truth always and yet appears to be reaching forth into that which is even a greater light, and a greater concept of Being.

Emerging from this light are many new symbols. These symbols would be partaking of Earth's truths. They would partake of Earth's truths in that they would carry certain symbols of the past, but they are carrying that which is new information and new insight.

Each symbol is embedded with information.
Each symbol is embedded in the DNA.
Each symbol is a carrier of various atoms of
      intelligence and awakening power em-
      bedded in the timelessness of your DNA.

For each perception then that would hold that symbol, a certain atom of intelligence and awakening power would be vitalized within them. All atoms of life now must be revitalized with God's Love and Power. And there are many ways to do this.

Through the symbols of old, they shall be revitalized. You shall see these symbolic truths and you shall use the old Masters and their teachings to bring forth new understandings and new perceptions. We would have you to look at the Yud, the Vov, and the Heh. We would have you to understand each of these symbols separately. We would have you to understand their symbolic meanings as they have been traditionally understood. We would have you to place them into new formulas, into new geodimensional forms, into those things that are interdimensional and not just on a flat space. We would have you to see them blazing with fire and we would see you therefore bringing forth a new teaching, and that is the teaching of materialization. It is the teaching of bringing that which is formed out of the atoms of heaven into the atoms of material existence.

These two atoms, although alike in basic form and essence, have of their particular purpose differences of opinion, due to the nature of Earth and to the nature of Heaven. It is now time for all of the atoms of Earth to be revitalized.

For this there will be new symbols borne out of the old, that will bring forth new teachings and rearrange the molecular structure of the very components of the Earth. These atoms will bring forth the true message of Heaven. And they will speak through the DNA and transform your very bodies.

And they will carry the Living Light of Form. And they will magnify their name, and it shall materialize on Earth even as it is in Heaven. These shapes will cause certain changes in the molecular components of all things surrounding it. And indeed we refer to it not only as a form, but literally as a Being of Light. For as you would understand, these are living symbols, and the atoms which they carry are living intelligences. Each one being an angel of God emerging forth out of the great Archangel Ezekiel.

And so we say to you then, "All of these forms are emerging as New Knowledge and New Teachings." And just as has occurred on many occasions in earth's past, a new vibration of teaching is being emitted out of the great Archangel of Light, Ezekiel. And so you will work with the Violet Flame and you will work with all that is termed of New Teachings. And you will work with that which are the

Masters of old and their symbols and you will bring forth new teachings out of that . . .

MERLIN:

What are we attempting to provide here? It is that which is termed a structural change. What are the structural changes? The building blocks of the past, the genetic codes of the past are re-evolving. They are re-emerging. Now— Ezekiel spoke to you of that which is termed the intelligence—the atom. I want to describe to you something that is most important to understand. There is the mirror of the Soul, and I am going to use Soul with a capital "S". The form of Soul that is perfected.

A perfected Soul has all energy and intelligence within it. It knows precisely who it is and what it wants. Deep, hidden beneath the genetic code there is a mirror soul. We could call this the atom of the DNA. The atom of the DNA has a personality that is indeed a mirror image to the macrocosm of the Soul, it is the microcosm. The atom and the Soul are indeed identical.

> At the structural level of the DNA we will then
> find certain amino acids and proteins
> and that sort of thing surrounding this
> mirror image.
> As though it were the garment that the mirror
> image carries or wears.

The mirror image, however, carries the truth.
The garment does not.
It is composed of many threads of thoughts
      composed by that DNA's ancestral
      karma.

At this time, you are awakening within each individual in your group, the Soul. The perfected Soul is now being drawn forth.

As you are achieving your own perfection,
      your perfection vibrates.
It vibrates in such a way to wake up a similar
      vibration within others, irrespective of
      what you say, irrespective of what you
      do, irrespective of who they are, what
      they say, or what they do.

The vibrational communication that exists from one Soul to another is always complete. And whether it is that that other Soul is awakened in a physical form or asleep, does not matter. That Soul will wake up. As it begins to wake up, it creates an awakening process for the mirror Soul.

The mirror Soul lies hidden beneath the many threads of DNA. Those threads can now be viewed as though they were literally being torn apart or opened up. Certain portions of the chemistry of the body are going to be affected by this. There is a substance that affects the DNA directly that has not yet been discovered by your Earth scientists. This substance is that which is the composition of thoughts. The composition of thoughts buried beneath the amino acids of the DNA code.

Soon, they will begin to discover this substance in connection with the AIDS research. It is part of the task of the AIDS scientists and researchers, to discover this substance. As they begin to discover it, they will understand that it is unlike any substance they have heretofore discovered, for it is changeable. It always changes. It is like thoughts, they generate new ones.

These substances are being released already in the body as the vibrations of the Earth shift. The more present the active Soul is within a physical structure, the more present the mirror Soul is within the DNA. The more present the mirror Soul is within the DNA, the more of a contrast occurs between that which it is and the DNA itself. Therefore there are substances being released from the DNA all the time.

These substances sometimes carry the element of fire. When they carry the element of fire, it will bring forth anger and other forms of negative emotions from the human body. Those negative emotions are simply being the outgrowth or outproduct from that which is being released in the element of fire.

The substances surrounding the DNA

will be according to each of the five major elements. As you understand each of those elements then, you will understand the substances that are being released into the physical system. It can always be traced back to the physical, but it will have its expression outwardly.

Fire is in a sense related to that which is termed of anger, angered belief, frustrations. I could also say the burning off of old beliefs through the element of fire, the consuming of them. At times they will be irrational, at times most rational. It doesn't matter. It is all being released in that way. They then need to be given a tangible outlet for that release, and more importantly, they need to be given a surrounding cushion of light. This you are providing for them [that body chemistry, or substance, that is the composition of thoughts]. It is a safe arena for them to release their fire. The substances that have been pulsing through their body and not being able to find a proper outlet— for they have captivated them in the body—are now being given an opportunity for that release. Let your sessions be as irrational as they like. And they will take a turn at times for irrationality—but that's all right, that's permitted.

There are other forms that are quite similar in nature. One is akash.

Akashic substance, when it is released from the body, has another form of intelli-

gence.
This form of intelligence is more wise.
It is more based upon that which in normally
        called the etheric body.

The body that is just a few inches above the skin, that most ones refer to as the blue aura? And that blue aura that exists just a few inches or in some cases just a quarter of an inch over the skin, seems to be a more atomical structure, as in automaton—hmmm? It is like a composition of electrical current.

Here lies the meridians and the acupuncture points, to some extent, some of the nadi's, but nadi's are different than meridians. They exist on every level of the Soul, on every dimension of the subtle bodies. They pass through dimensions as opposed to meridians that lay within each dimension separately.

When it is that this Soul is activating the
        substance of akash, there will be more
        of a spacial change in terms of their
        physical structure.
The spacial change in the physical structure is
        due to more pure intelligence or pure
        thoughts at the basis of their etheric
        body.

Where there are jam ups, then you will need to lay on hands. You can do this directly, or it would be best to have the group do this directly. You will sense more intelligence—more space involved in the perception of the individual.

You must be very keen, however. You must learn to study the elements. Learn to feel them and to sense them, so that in some way you have a model to detect them. And that way you will detect what's going on in each individual. If you were to discover that it was akash indeed that was being affected, you could ask, "Is it akash?". And you will get confirmation.

Perhaps it is only a marginal confirmation, and you would want to say, "Is it akash and air? Are the two working together here?" You might say, "Yes, that's what it is then." Then we'll work in that way, and I'll describe that to you in a moment.

But if it is simply akash, this is the way you would work: Akash demands touch. It *demand*s touch. The meridians could be stimulated, you could have individuals sense pressure points. They would want to look to those areas where the energy wants to move, but cannot, because it is blocked. They will look at the body, perhaps in the shoulders. Shoulders are very common these days for most individuals are carrying a lot of responsibility. So neck and shoulders would be very common. Also shoulders moving in to the arm sockets. For there is where one reaches out and carries the responsibility, tries to do or to change, so the pressure around the shoulder blades and in the arm sockets would be very appropriate. Just apply pressure, sending love. That would help to heal.

If it is involved with air, and it's a mixture between akash and air, air is thoughts in motion—like the wind. It is also associated with the breath. These are thoughts that want to move into action. They are not just part of the basic structure, like akash is part of the basic structure—the way one perceives oneself, the dimensions of oneself. The air element is one that is the thoughts in motion, actually wanting to create change and expand. Here one would ask to simply control the breath. Through deep breathing they could then go through various transformations.

You might in this case use some re-birthing techniques for instance. Or just simple breathing techniques: Having them lay upon the floor with others sitting around them and perhaps everyone breathing synchronously with the major individual that is going through the change. Here is where you need to trust that everyone present is going through the same thing, but one being more of an outlet than another. So have all sit about the one as he is laying about the floor and breathing. And everyone just breathes together. At the end, you might begin to share insights if you like.

You can bring the thoughts up into form and express them and experience them. But the main trouble with this is that thoughts tend to lock one into a reality, when in truth, the *vayu* element, or that element of breath and air wants to move and expand. So let the breath expand, rather than the thoughts that tend to lock in [to reality]. Do you understand?

Now, I've already explained the element of fire, for that is the next. When air begins to move and expand to such a degree that it begins to push against the old beliefs, then it does release anger, which is fire. Air moves into fire, akash moves into air. And as the fire begins to be activated, that's when you can start to release your irrational thoughts and feelings, particularly the shouting kinds of things, and using pillows or whatever it is that you would need to allow for that kind of release.

The next is the element of water. Water is more smooth than fire. And as that which is the fire has been released, the elements of emotions start to calm down. They are already starting to integrate, there is sadness that begins to come up, and there is more of a willingness to accept love. There is more love flowing. As love starts to flow, it naturally creates integration.

So, when one is in that period of sadness, first you must check to make sure that the other side is cleared, the fire element. If it has been completely cleared, then you can move on and create love. If it has not been, then you must shift the individual out of their sadness into that which is probably fear first and then anger resulting from that.

And now let us move on with the water, for water is one of the most important elements of connection today. The water element is going to create into physical structure, into the very muscles of the body. The muscles are fed by the blood. When you start to exercise, the muscles get pumped up with blood. That is the water element. The sadness, or water element, is going to fill up the individual, integrate the new energy that is trying to come from their higher self through the mirror Soul that is underneath the DNA. The water element is a good element and can be reinforced with much Love.

Have others about them comfort them—ask the individual what they want to feel in order to feel comforted. Do you want to feel love? Do you want to feel loved by your mother? Do you want to feel loved by so and so ...? Then have someone in the group represent mother to them and say what they need to hear. Give comfort, tell them the things they need to hear. *Give comfort.* That will heal and soothe and integrate the water element.

The final element is that of Earth. The Earth will only be in place once Heaven is in place. That's simply the truth. The Earth otherwise will shake all over the place until it is finally in place. But Earth is borne out of water and, therefore, borne out of love. Heaven can only integrate into Earth when love is fully in place and accepted. Once it is accepted, then Earth is stable. So the Earth element then is not just the giving of love, but absolutely accepting it as peace. The Earth element will be the last. When the Earth element releases from the DNA, in truth what is taking place is the transition from the third dimension into the fourth and fifth dimensions. There the physical structure of the DNA no longer needs to be clothed with all these false garments. The old thoughts of the ancestors can now transform into pure changeable essence of light remaining coherent and appearing to be solid, like the Earth appears to be solid, but is actually not dense, but full of light, and transparent.

In truth, the Earth element, which on this plane [of] third dimension, appears solid—in the fourth and fifth dimensions becomes transparent. When Earth finally begins to be released from the DNA, in that stage of emotional releasing or physical releasing, it will always become transparent. Even though it appears as Earth, which is peaceful and stable, it will be transparent as though it appears stable on one hand, [but] the truth is, that it is like the akash, it is transparent and always moving. But moving within itself so coherently, that it appears to be stable.

This is a new teaching, a new understanding. You can apply it in whatever way you want. These are symbols, they are old symbols, they are in every tradition of the Earth— these elements. They have been there at the basis of all sciences and every tradition for a reason. They are at the basis of it all. They are that which clothes the Soul. By understanding them, you can bring out the teachings that are now the new. This is perhaps what Ezekiel was trying to say to you when he was saying, "Look to the Masters of old to bring out the new teachings."

Q: How does this healing spread to the rest of the world?

A: That happens automatically. The cells are like receiver dishes—you know—like those for radios. If one station emits a signal, it can be passed on from microwave dish to microwave dish. It is a similar phenomenon with the human DNA. When you build up a spiritual charge, as you are doing, you literally create spiritual transformation in the structure of the DNA. The DNA is a vibration. Indeed, it is a vibration that is transmitting information all the time. All of the cells of the body are in constant contact with each other through this device of vibration from the DNA. This is another area that the scientists will begin to discover— how the cells actually communicate. Not just through the blood or through the nervous system, but through actual radio waves of cells from one cell to the other. This is going on all the time in the body. It's how if one cell begins to heal itself, the other cells that are in the same organ begin to heal themselves. It is occurring by the vibrational communication.

The accelerated vibration of truth is more powerful than the lesser vibration of untruth. That accelerated vibration takes precedence and, therefore, is more communicated to the cell than those that are untruths. This is true not just within the human body, but in all other bodies. In truth all you need to do is bring in that essence, that spiritual power, the spiritual charge, and start the transformation in the cells in your bodies. Then those signals will go out. First to your relatives and friends—those that are most associated and most like you in vibration. Their cells will receive the information first. Then, that gets transmitted around the world—literally. It is what you call the theory of the hundredth monkey. It only takes one to begin a change, and the rest of the cells can continue it.

The transmissions themselves are ones of highly charged atoms of vibrational ideas. These ideas are not composed of thoughts as you understand them. They are atoms of information on a vibrational level—impulses of pure intelligence in its undistorted form. You can say that they are geometric like an atom. These geometric bundles of intelligence are projected through the akash, or ether, like a wave through water. They do not require tissue in order to be transmitted. They can literally be transmitted through the air. Any like cellular structure will pick them up, just as a radio signal is picked up.

Now, if you want to make this process more powerful as a healer, then you simply become aware of all these microwave dishes. You become aware of the broadcast signals and reinforce those signals to send a clearer and more powerful direct message. What you are literally doing is you are adding a message to what is already being sent. You are sending a thought form, a healing thought form, perhaps an affirmation, along with the geometric bundle of information already being sent. Ask the Soul Deva for an affirmation that is appropriate to be sent with the thought waves already in motion. In this way, you are working in perfect synchrony with the body's natural processes.

Q: Merlin, could you discuss longevity and death?
A: You see—God did not create death—mankind

did! Let me explain this to you because I see how you struggle with these concepts . . . all right?

God created the etheric body, a body of perfect light. No distortion anywhere. It was complete in itself and created out of God's eternal substance. This is what your Bible meant when it said that you were created out of God's image. The flame of light that God took to create you was the same substance as the flame of His great body of light that we refer to as the Central Sun. So the flame is the same as the sun from which it came. It carries all of the same qualities. This Flame of Light is your natural condition, your Light Body, as it is often called.

The story of Adam and Eve in the Garden of Eden is the story of the light body in its original condition as God created it for each of you. He gave to you all of the qualities that He had, and offered to you all of the fruits of His creation (the Garden of Eden).

He said to you, "Taste of any fruit in My Garden. It's all yours! But there is one fruit that I recommend that you do not eat, that is the fruit of the knowledge of good and evil, which will bring you unhappiness all of the rest of your days. It is the only fruit in My Garden that is not sweet."

It was the knowledge of good and evil that brought about the fall. As a result of that, mankind began to create limitations, rights and wrongs—all sorts of rights and wrongs, right down to where you're supposed to look this way and not that way. These thought energies began to condense around the original eternal flame that God gave as your Light Body, and weigh it down.

You see—originally on Earth, a Being could appear however they wished. They could change their form at will. They could fly through the air. They could do all manner of what you would call miracles today.

> Whatever they desired they could do!
> Why?
> God created them to be like God, to be in the
>   image of God.
> And there was no death.
> The only judgements that God gave to the
>   world were *good* and *very good*.
> That's all!

Death was created later as a result of the limitations which mankind placed on itself. Your bodies became denser and denser, as the limited thought forms created out of good and evil condensed around you.

At first they slowed the rate of vibration of the etheric body down to exist for maybe 150,000 years. Then the etheric body experienced its first letting go of the weight of its thought forms. An experience which you later would refer to as death.

Death is just the experience of releasing the

weight of old thought forms that have limited your existence.

In later times, such as Atlantis, a Being might live 1,000 to 10,000 years. Even in your scriptures, all over the world, you have the stories of Beings who lived for centuries. But today you are lucky if you live to be a hundred. So much weight you carry around unneccessarily!

You see the increasing limitation upon the Earth? Now—God did not create this, you did! Each time that you limit yourself you create an armor about your etheric body that slows you down, you feel it as an encumbrance.

Now what is this etheric body that we speak of? On a cellular level it is the Soul Deva! Surrounding the Soul Deva are all of the limited thought forms, condensed vibrational patterns that later evolved into the threads of genetic patterning called DNA. As you learn to release these limiting thought forms from your DNA, you will spontaneously create longevity. Time will disappear and all encumbrances and limitations will dissolve!

Blessings to you! This is your gift from Heaven! Heaven's doors have always been open to you, and now you are choosing to enter them again to experience your original inheritance.

Blessings . . . and welcome to you!

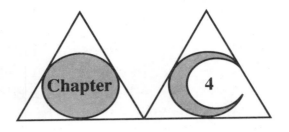

JESUS' ASCENSION

By Ascended Master Sananda
(Jesus the Christ)

My final release occurred while it was that I was yet upon the cross. For in that moment of transfiguration—in that moment when I was finally released from this body—I saw a challenge. In the moment just prior to my death, I recognized that my human form and my personality as Jesus had not yet fulfilled of its nature.

And I called forth as I looked out upon all those who had already forgotten of my teachings, and I felt helpless, for I felt their pain and their suffering, and I had not yet fulfilled them. And I called forth and I said, "My God, why hast thou forsaken me?"

It had not yet ended. In that moment, I thought, *my responsibility was not yet complete.*

Then I recognized that there were storm clouds brewing. And that the lightening and majesty of God was all about me. And that darkness had begun to descend upon the Earth.

In that moment I recognized I am not of darkness, but of Light. And that my will and my intention are not my own, but of God's. And here I chose to resume my Full Power. And I was liberated.

An angel of Light came to take me, and assist me with my Ascension process. In that moment I recovered my true duty to life, which was not to carry the responsibility of the world upon my shoulders, but to give it to God.

And in that moment I realized that indeed my purpose was being fulfilled, even while I doubted. And that my vision had included a vision of my role in my personality and in my human form in connection to all living things. And I was in error.

That in truth, God was in form. God moved through me in mysterious ways—ways that I could not comprehend. Ways far greater than my human mind could understand.

I had become possessive of the work which I
was to accomplish for God.

And yet in that moment I was capable of releasing. And the angel inside of me then departed of this human form and moved up into Heaven. And there I was re-educated as to the true nature of all of life.

As I returned to this human form, when it was in the tomb, I remembered that form of light. And this human form was lifted in a moment, out of death, even into that which was pure light and lightness. It was lifted up into the very air and suspended there.

It was as though in a magical instant every cellular transformation possible had taken place. And all the elements of untruth and limitation were released and there was no more death in it. But only the life force, majesty, and living flow of God.

There was no humanity remaining within it that was not in God's power. And I had surrendered this will even upon the cross.

Now here I was, and every angel was dancing within me. Every cell was alive with life force and I stood forth.

I alighted from the table and stood forth in the tomb. Once again I was faced with a challenge. How, in my light body, was I to remove such a great stone as covered the face of the tomb? How was I to move? How was I to pass out of that condition?

For I was not yet fully involved with Light, though I was in *Truth*. Memory of my physical existence yet overshadowed me.

And I thought that perhaps I would surrender. And in that moment of surrendering I called upon two angels of God to do the work for me, and lift the stone from the tomb. And this they did quite easily.

In each and every case I recognized that now my relationship was such as to command all that I would wish out of God in me. That God's mighty angels would fulfill all of my destiny for me.

It was my pleasure then to glide in the power
      of God!
I use this expression "to glide in the power of
      God", for I did not walk upon the Earth.
But I walked in the Heaven of Earth.
And, therefore, I glided.
There was no effort involved.
For there was no resistance where one lives in
      God.
In Truth.
There is no resisting Power!

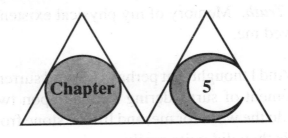

MEDITATION ON ASCENSION

By Ascended Lady Master Mother Mary

I AM Mary, and I welcome you in peace.

I present to you my White Dove and my White
    Flame.
For in the Dove is the Flame of Life.
It is the Flame of Peace.
It is the Flame of Love and Ascension
    Power.

I place my White Flame now, upon your brow.
That the Dove may spread its wings.
And that the inner mind may be opened, and a
    divine attunement may occur.

There the spreading of the white light, like the
    wings of the Dove, lift you into a higher
    realm of understanding and wakeful-
    ness.
In this awakening power there is peace, and it
    is all pervasive, spreading everywhere.

Now—I place my hand upon your heart, and
    therein, to place a seed.
This seed is in the form [of] a cross.

It is like the fairy cross of olde, for it has
    magical power.
It is the horizontal and vertical planes of life.
And it is the Balance:

Its vertical staff of life, drawing deep within
    the Earth, the Red Flame.
While its upper wings reach to the Dove and
    spread into Heaven as white Light.

Its horizontal limbs reach from right to left,
    from male to female, in perfect balance,
    for both stretch evenly and equally.
Therein the seed is planted, deep in the heart.

The heart feels its presence as it would expand
deep into the Earth, and reach high into
Heaven.
Sharing its two arms of love, that's male and
female with all parts of the body now.

Therein I place my Child, Lord Jesus, the
Healer.
I place the Child deep within the Cross (not
upon the Cross, but within it), as an even
tinier seed of Light, like an atom . . .
a Gold Pearl,
a Gold Star,
the Star of Bethlehem.

The announcing of Ascension and the transformation of the crude values of Earth
into the refined values of Heaven.

Therein I place my seed of Love, deep in His
Heart, within the Core of the Gold Pearl.

Now— let His presence and love shine all
about you.

This Gold Pearl becomes a Gold Sun, the
Central Sun, for He is the Sun of God.
And God, therefore, dwells within Him as He
dwells in all living things.

May the Central Sun now bring its warmth
    until it is a great globe of golden Light,
    of perfect warmth, harmony, and peace,
    and the deepest quality of divine Love.

Now—let this globe of light, this Great Sun,
    warm you.
May its warmth literally fill your chest with
    Love and Harmony.
And may there be felt therein, perfection.
Perfection of God's Love and God's Will.
And may the questioning mind be released from
    its need to question or to understand,
As God's revealing power lies within the heart
    and the Golden Sun.

Through this Sun there is created a rainbow.
The rainbow arcs out into the lungs, and there
    the lungs would breathe the seven
    colors of the rainbow.

As the lungs would breathe the seven colors of
    the rainbow arcing from the Central
    Sun,
You would find the breath becoming fulfilled,
    its gray area becoming luminous.

Indeed the rainbow is formed from the mois-
    ture in the lungs,
As the Golden Light would pass upon it,

thus forming the rainbow.
And all of that which is moist and warm within
the lungs now becomes healed with the
golden Light of the Sun and the rainbow
colors as they reach into the body.

First into the spine, and then, like a prism, as
the colors of the rainbow touching the
spine begin to spread apart
Each one moving to their appropriate chamber,
The Chamber of Light of the human chakras.

As you would continue to breathe, breathe into
the spine allowing the currents of light
from the rainbow to spread into all the
Earthly chakras

The currents of light would then, in turn, each
bring a Sun of light into the chakras
Each of these Suns of light, formed from the
great golden Sun, becomes each of the
colors of the rainbow
In each center it is Gold, and carries the Gold
Pearl.

Within the color of the rainbow Sun, where the
Gold Pearl was first perceived,
You will perceive a great temple, a Golden
Temple, a Temple of great perfection.

This is the *I AM Presence*, and its chamber of
knowledge from the causal body.

This is the chamber of wisdom, that wishes to
express itself freely and fully to each
chamber of the chakras.

Each chakra of the body is a temple of perception,
Adulterated by the human karma that it has
accumulated.

This human karma has been dislodged, and it
is rest less in the body,
It wishes to be removed from the body, for it is
the body's karma and not the Soul's.

These great Suns of rainbow light, each
moving to their appropriate places,
Dislodging this karma permanently and
establishing therein a Temple of Heaven
for your *I AM Presence*.

As this phenomenon continues to occur, there
will be a need for releasing and for
cleansing:

First, we would ask you to take regular salt
baths, warm enough that the body is
soothed, but not so hot as to stir it.

In that soothing salt bath, you would add a touch of lemon.

This would help to free the body of its ailments of ego, of the misqualified energy of cancer,

And of those things from which the body's toxins have accumulated.

We would ask you to do this for three weeks.

Prior to each bath, you should meditate as we have just given you.

Allow the energies to pass through your body once again, as I have just done for you as I spoke these words.

Next, following the three weeks, you will begin three more weeks of rose water baths with the salt.

As you add the salt and rose water mixed into the bath, there shall be a soothing, for it shall be My Rose.

When you would add the rosewater to the salt water, you will bless it.

Visualize my form in the bottle, pouring a tablespoon or two into the water (that would be enough, for such is My Power).

As such, I will give to you this gift, that your heart might open, and that you might more fully and consciously ascend.

Prior to each Ascension process, there is discipline.

The discipline has to do with each Soul's final mission upon the Earth.

You are to engage in this process whole heartedly and completely.

Each of the baths will be considered as a cleansing in preparation,

As though cleansing the body and purifying it for its final admission into Heaven.

During in this process, you will discover that certain wave frequencies of light are responsible for the cleansing of the entire body,

For the body is composed of Light.

All of what we have given to you today is sequential.

It is sequenced into the perfect synchrony of cleansing the body in preparation for Ascension.

This is a tool for Ascension

Use it as our gift to you, and bless others with it, as you are to ascend with others.

The collective groups of light will work together to create the breakthroughs for the planet Earth.

And all will ascend together.

My Love must pour through the Earth that the brightness of God may shine in all human hearts together.

All of My Love,
Mary

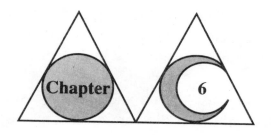

A MESSAGE FROM HEAVEN

By Ascended Master Sananda
(Jesus the Christ)

Selah—so shall it be! And so shall it be. As your will is in Heaven, so shall it be on Earth. But this is the challenge before you, is it not? That the will in Heaven be heard on the Earth, so may you walk as one of us. May that light within you shine and may your voice be heard, even over the towering voices that may cry out. For in this time there is much assistance gathering and there is a need to receive that assistance.

Indeed, we are hopeful. For it appears as though the Earth is finally ready. But we are awaiting and watchful for that proper moment to present itself in which all of humanity might ascend. And that day is surely and truly coming. As it was in the beginning, releasing and for taking hold—taking hold of that which you call the moment, "seize the moment" they say, so shall it be in the end—Om Selah.

"Tat tvam asi", is an ancient expression meaning: Thou art that, all that is thou art, all that is to become thou art. And lest you forget of this, we say to you, "Your heart shall remain strong and your eyes true. So allow that, that the heart sees, to be known by the heart and to be accepted and experienced by the heart, for that is your keystone, the cornerstone from which all of the foundation of future belief shall be constructed."

There is no greater foundation upon the Earth; not in its soil, or its mountains, or its oceans—for the human heart is all of these things. It is composed of the soil of the Earth, it is the mountain of forgiveness, and it is the ocean of belief. And so, it must be seen that the heart shall triumph over all things and then the Living God [will] present itself from the human heart to the human spirit. For as yet the human spirit considers itself one, and God another–but this gap, too, is closing. And the separation that once appeared endless, is now completing.

But in this process, there shall be much trial and tribulation in the human experience. And there must be forgiveness—an ocean of it. And that ocean must circulate through all the veins that it might return to the heart. For what emerges, must return. So what is given forth to another, must be received by one's own dear Self. In this, then, there is true forgiveness; otherwise, it is pointless action, for it is a point that wanders and does not return.

But so it has been, that the Earth has gazed upon itself and it has learned. It has been taught many things, but each teacher has their own point of view, and now all must come together. There is forgiveness in this process that must be heard. For it is through the agency of forgiveness, that fear is dissipated.

Without forgiveness, there will be fear.
There is no fear in forgiveness.
Forgiveness is for giving—forgiving,
For releasing and for taking hold,
Taking hold of that which you call the mo-
    ment, "seize the moment", [as] they say.

In this the heart is responsive and knowledgeable. And yet, how much, how often, the heart would be embedded with fear? And in that moment, all becomes lost until the next moment arrives. In this there is separation between the human spirit and God's will. But you are quickly, you are swiftly—like the wings of eagles and like the wings of doves—learning.

And so the challenge is presented to you, and
    to all the Earth.
To return to your Father who art in Heaven,
    and to your Mother who art in Earth,

And to the combination of the two and their
    product,
The prodigal Sons and Daughters who dwell in
    the human spirit, and who coalesce in
    the heart.

We welcome you who are in Heaven and we who are
of Spirit. For your spiritual needs are your Earthly ones.
And your Earthly needs are our spiritual desires. This is a
rather complex subject, in that Earth has little understanding
in this regard. But it is called the triumph of the spirit and
the leadership of the Soul—the true Soul, and not the
embodied one. For in that which is termed the Earthly
needs, their desires, and their unwelcome nature, then there
is healing and forgiveness, a forgiveness and healing which
brings home the point that once wandered endlessly.

All human karma must be forgiven in order
    that it might return home.
A feast has been already prepared for it, by
    those of us in Heaven.
It is welcomed then, for the feet of karma to
    swiftly return.
And wherever they would walk, we would be
    there waiting to receive them.
The banquet table now appears barren, but we
    hear rumors to the effect that the Sons
    and Daughters of God are returning.
And so we would prepare and welcome them
    with a mighty feast.

So shall it be, for such is the proclamation of
Heaven and Lord God—Malech Ha
Olam—Himself/Herself.

And with the Father/Mother God, the children of the
Earth of Light shall return home. And they shall bear in their
hands their brother and their sister, for by the hand they shall
lead them, as a shepherd his flock. And the sheep are not
often willing to return home to the stable, for they would yet
wish to graze awhile longer; they do not know of the feast
that has been prepared for them, far greater than any field
of endeavor.

But they must be taught, they must be trained. They
must be led Heavenward, for the gates of Heaven have
already opened unto them, and they, from their side, have
opened to the gates of Heaven. Why then, won't they
return?

For the children of Earth, habits run deep. This is an
assumption that you have made about yourselves that is not
true. And yet you possess of it, as if it were your mother and
your father, and then you perceive of it in their forms, and
in those of your brothers and your sisters.

All of this of course, is but an illusion, a mirage. An
appearance before your very eyes that does not exist, in that
it does not need to exist. For the veil which separates you,
is a veil that is not of Heaven, but of Earth, and Earthly made.
But it is also Earthly undone. That is why it be Heaven-

made. The consequence of such activity is such:

As to beam Heaven, Earthward,
And to beam Earth, Heavenward.
Thus, you see your six pointed star and the
meaning of the tri-grams.
It is to be possessed of the human spirit.
Its divine location in the physical form is the
heart center.
There it would radiate outward into all centers,
were all centers willing to receive it.

But here we must pause, and examine, why it is that such an important message is not easily received. The heart would be vocal were the throat to allow it. The mind would be attentive to the infinite and to intuitive perception, were the perceptions themselves not to be placed in their categories.

The structure of human life permits only more structure and not the infinite charm of wisdom. Not to mention those things, that are possessed of the flesh, for now we speak only of that which is termed of the spirit. But the fleshly persuasions, and the truths of the human body and its form, are also but a mirage. For that which exists as infinite in Heaven, knows no veil. It knows no persuasion either, for it simply *is*. It knows no coming or, no going. For it is come and it has gone—already.

It is present with all knowledge, even where you would go. Why bother then, you say? For if we know all of this in Heaven, what are our excuses made of on Earth?

And again we respond, "A mirage." But a mirage is often perceived as real. It is not easily understood, even by the wise. For what is perceived, yet strikes upon the senses, activates them and their preconceived persuasions, their intellectual inclinations. All of this of course also, is a mirage—to be released into the infinite arms of Heaven.

To do this one needs only surrender their whole and their will, their form and the formless into their very own hearts—the heart that possesses the wheel of fortune, the Sacred Wheel, with six points, the seventh, being its axis. So—two tri-grams, one above and one below, each pointed toward the other, each overlapping each other—a merger of identity—thus forming a new union and a new perception. For when one looks upon Heaven with the eyes of Earth, and one peers back at Earth with the eyes of Heaven, then one truly understands.

And so, allow this tri-gram and its brother, to increase in size until it would encompass all that which you term your human form. Those that are its upper points, would be made of the neck and shoulders with outstretched arms. Those that would be seen as its lower would be understood as a base that spread apart at the knees and the hips. As you would be seen then in an inclined position, as though seated [cross legged], you would then understand that reaching forth from these points, each itself as a star, is the star of Heaven in the mind, the star of Earth in the feet, the star of your right and your left, your east and your west, with your two hands.

And thus you would notice two more that you do not yet understand. And they would simply be called: Embrace and be willing. And out of this, then, comes a third tri-gram, and that which comes from Heaven. What is this energy from Heaven? You have termed this energy *goddess*, and you have termed it well. You have also termed this energy *spirit* and you have also termed it well. You have termed it *awakening*, a *pulsing*, a *quickening*, and you have also termed it well for it is all of these things and much more.

But out of this awakening shall come a new force. It is literally the force of Heaven in Earth, and Earth in Heaven. The third tri-gram represents the product of the two: It is the gift from Heaven called: The Miraculous. Many sages have spoken of this event but have not been so clear up to now, as you three shall be. What is the three? That which comes into you: Father, Son and Holy Spirit. For as that merges with your identity, your personal form becomes transformed into light, and into its full stretch and expanse of Heaven.

So, it must be said, that your own form itself will resist this process due to the mirage it has felt about itself, its own personal identity, persuasion, inclination, persistence. But as its persistence is worn thin, out of the great light beyond illusion, there shall be called a Triumph of Spirit, and there shall be seen a triumph of the Soul, in the body, in full awakening, with a triad in full golden light. It is a spiritualization of all matter, in all forms, densities and conditions. It is when spirit finally returns home, with its labors of love possessed of the suitcase of knowledge of material form and existence.

As it passes through the window or door of perception of Heaven, it perceives a tri-gram of most radiant light. Some have called this the golden triad. It is a window through which all knowledge can be known, for it is through this window that each spirit must pass once it has completed of its matter. Then those things that truly matter, are embedded in subtle light form and condition in the very walls of the tri-gram, the window of perception. The gateway to Heaven then is known as a gate of many gates, and many corridors of knowledge—this is the *miraculous*.

In truth, there is but one triad: Father, Son and Holy Ghost merely representing that triad in an Earthly manner, a manner in which you might perceive and understand of its condition. But what is the Father, the Son, and Holy Ghost? The Ghost is that which moves, it is a Ghost because in truth, it does not move—it remains silent. The silent figure that represents the Heavenly Father, is that which stands beyond all creation and its form. And the Spirit of God passes through this form.

When it would recognize itself, then it is termed the Son of God; a child borne of its dual form of existence, the silent (the Father) and the Holy Ghost. Out of that, then is possessed a new spirituality and understanding, a condition for which can only be understood through Earthly existence as you would call it, though it would be in all dimensions everywhere, in all planetary conditions, and star conditions.

And out of that Holy Spirit and Heavenly Father there is again borne a union within the Son; and that Son becomes effulgent (bright, shining, brilliant), for the Sons and Daughters of God are all self-effulgent and yet conditional upon the play of the Mother/Father God within them; the condition and the conditionless. As this would suit you, we would possess of ourselves to yield further understanding.

This understanding is in the form of a robe bearing the six-pointed star. This robe is placed about you in the form of a seamless garment. It is what can be cherished as one's own Ascension garment, for such was the garment of Christ as he wore the shroud, as he ascended into Heaven— his own garment [the physical body] having been replaced by more fragrant ones.

So shall it be, that as the six-pointed star is emblazoned upon this garment, so shall it be that the Soul, or Son or Daughter of God shall see it and shall understand—it is the merger of the Self in motion and its silent witness.

That is the keystone of all understanding and
the possession of all wisdom—everywhere.
That which you are exists in Heaven, though

you do not know it.
That which you shall become, shall know it
and exist in Heaven and on Earth, at the
same time.

As this moment then passes forward—through time
and through space—that knowledge passes forward with it
and there is an opening. That opening is created by the
Living God—its motion is the Holy Ghost or Holy Spirit
through the individual will, [and] there it is discovered that
the individual will possess the miraculous.

My blessings to you . . . for receiving this disser-
tation on Truth, on the Sacred Star, and on the Emblem of
Truth of the Seamless Garment. I AM he whom you would
term Sananda: Sa-ananda (Jesus the Christ).

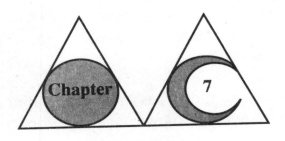

THE VISION OF APOCALYPSE— ARMAGEDDON

By Ascended Master Merlin

Yes—well, blessings be to each and every one of you! It is I, it is the Merlin. And today I wish to address the difficult and most complex of the New Age—Armageddon. Yes, the Apocalypse . . . the Earth changes . . . the doom and gloom, as they say. The catastrophes, and all of that which is to either transpire or not transpire, according to your interpretation. Ah—yes, there are many, aren't there?

All of those out there, saying *this* and *that*.

All of those up here, saying *this* and *that*. Well—who is right—what is going on?

Let me start out by saying first of all that, "Those of Earth are biased according to their religions, and their religious beliefs." This is natural, of course, for they have only the dogmatic teachings of their ancestors to go by. For indeed most of them have the lack of perception to truly see clearly into that which is called the Apocalypse.

Some have had their own visions, indeed. But from whence has this vision come? Has it not come out of fear and trembling, as it were? Out of the fear of God, rather than the love of God? Well—in that case then there is the Light of Truth shining through fear. In which case we would say that, that interpretation will be colored by fear, even though it shares in the light of truth. We must caution you, therefore, to recognize where fear abounds on Earth. And, of course, when you are truly one with God, there is no fear, for all is knowingness, and all of love. God is a loving God, after all, not a God of punishment.

And that leads us into where I am to begin. For in my association with other ascended Masters, and Beings of Light, we have learned that there is no such thing as death. That there is no such thing as doom and destruction. But, indeed, in the eyes of God, all is loving and peaceful.

Now, truly in the eyes of man it is quite different, as you well know. You have heard me lecture time and time again on the lessons of the Ascension process, and the higher self nature being perfect. You have heard me speak of the *Fall*. And other Masters speaking of that time in which the Earth condition truly became a condition, rather than an unlimited one. Conditional, filled with logic and dogmatic teachings, rights and wrongs. And, as the course of evolution took place, more and more of your teachings became teachings separated from truth.

You say, "But Merlin that's just your opinion, we have ours." So be it—so be it. But if we were to look at the universe [we would see that] there is indeed only one universe, and it is loving. However, you may create in that universe whatsoever you wish. And if you wish to put fear and destruction into it, then—so be it. And thus have you done since the beginning of time. And should you wish to continue in this manner of fear and destruction, what you would call repetitious lessons, and reincarnations, incarnation upon incarnation, to complete your Earthly karma—so be it. You will be given that opportunity, but not here on Earth.

You say, "Now wait a second Merlin, you said something there I don't understand." Well, this is quite simple. According to even your *Book of Revelations* and the other prophecies around the Earth, it is said that there will come a time of liberation. To the Hindus, that great being will be Kalki, and he will ride on white horse. As you will see, that is also the first horse of the horsemen of the Apocalypse, a white horse. And this being will be a shining Being of Light.

His first task will be to come and liberate the Solar Kings from their sleep. It is said that they are sleeping in eastern Europe, in a cave somewhere. This is the vision of the Hindus, and they [the Solar Kings] are the true leaders of the Earth. Which is now, according to their tradition, the Earth being ruled by the Shudra King—meaning those that are not fit for leadership. So be it—I believe we are describing this time period perfectly, aren't we?

Every tradition on Earth has a vision of a new order of life, coming at the end of time. Unfortunately, what has taken place in your world is a vision, or visions, of those who are of the male order of life and under the limitations of their own philosophies and insights. I must remind you, that all of you are under the limitations of your own knowledge and teachings, and the visionary portion of self, because the mind can only think according to the things that it knows. It doesn't just dream up its symbols. It must have something for a reference point and so it uses its own logic.

Well, so, in a world such as Nostradamus lived in, he had to speak in more poetic terms. The same way with Saint John and his vision. The same way with the Hindus, whether it be Vyasa or Shaunaka, or any of the great visionaries. We must say, that they all used the symbols of their time because that was the language that they understood. Unfortunately, as they projected into the end of time, into the beginning of the dawning of a new age, they couldn't see what was truly beyond. They could only say that what we knew as the limitations would be released and removed. To some, like Nostradamus, it looked like death. Through Saint John, on the other hand, it looked like mystery. But indeed, it was his path—for indeed as we shall discover, it was his own personal path of Ascension, as we shall shortly notice.

Well—let us then get into it. For we are at those time periods of the Earth when the end of time has come. This does not mean the end of everything. It means the beginning of a new order that does not recognize time and space in the same linear fashion in which you do today. It simply means that now we will be going by a new time scheme. Much like your physicists are discovering that the laws of Sir Isaac Newton are now somewhat out of date. For indeed, there is a new order and philosophy to the religion of physics. Oh yes, they are becoming quite conscious, those physicists. They are discovering that at the basis of it all is a mystery.

> An impermeable, impenetrable, overlying, complete field—unified mystery, beyond anything of their expectations.
> Where matter floats.
> Where liquids move upstream, instead of downstream.
> Where you tickle in one corner and, as one physicist says, it laughs over there, in the other corner—superfluidity, superconductivity.

And this is all just a beginning. It is a new age, my

friends, and we are about to begin a most exciting time in human history. Where all that which you have seen as human history will simply go *quite down the drain* as you have completed your showering off, and will begin now to enter into a new and more cleansed era.

> Human history will be cleansed.
> Those things that are no longer useful to mankind, will not simply be remembered—that's all.
> You will look upon those things that are useful to you, and discard those things that are not.

Well—let us begin with the vision of Saint John's, since in your western world at this time and age, that is the predominant thinking of the new age. I might add, that two thousand years ago much preparation went into that time period. It was understood that after four-and-one-half million years of human history, that we were entering the last sequence of life. The sequences of life, by the way, go in periods of about fourteen-thousand years. Seven cycles of two-thousand years each. As we shall discover, this number seven is most significant. We are now in one of the last seven cycles.

The two thousand years beginning with Christ, or Jesus, as you understand him, began the period of what we shall term the final cleansing, or clearing, of mankind. This actually will end a fourteen-thousand year cycle, and begin a two-thousand year cycle [in] which mankind will be in the process of changing not only their world view, but the physical composition of their matter. In the next five to ten years, it wiil be understood that we are completing a two-thousand year cycle since Jesus' time. This cycle has to be completed for all of mankind, not simply for one or two individuals. As we will see as we examine the *Book of Revelations* and its text, we shall see that in truth this is a period in which all of mankind has to make a choice between good and evil. Between Ascension, and resurrection, and death. Or what is so commonly put in the *Book of Revelations*—fire and brimstone. Well—we shall see what that means as well.

Let us begin then on our discussions. For as exciting as the next two-thousand year time period is, you cannot possibly understand it until you understand what is being completed here. Two thousand years ago all of what is to be completed here was understood. And it was also understood that mankind is somewhat stubborn. That you stubborn fellows and sisters out there are resistant of learning your lessons and, therefore, require a little bit of a boost. You also require some inspiration.

Jesus was chosen, out of all the Masters possible, to come to Earth to demonstrate Ascension. And then, not only to demonstrate it for himself, but to teach others the same process. As you know, Mother Mary also ascended, and so did Saint John and many of the other disciples. Since that time we have had other great lineages of the western world such as Saint Germain, also demonstrating this same process. [Also] Paul the Venetian, the great artist of the Renaissance. We have many, many such beings demonstrating Ascension.

We are concerned, at this time, with the words of Saint John. His words, as well as many of the other disciples, about the Ascension process and the life of Jesus, were meant to be stirred around the world. To stir up within the super conscious mind, the invisible mind of the human spirit, a recognition of a truth long forgotten by humanity. Prior to that time, for the most part, with the exception of certain place in Asia from time to time when there was a great Master, the knowledge of liberation was sparse. With the exception of certain principles here and there that would come to light in each tradition, the knowledge that one is linked to God was lost.

Even the followers of Moses proclaimed that it was Moses' unique gift to this Earth to have spoken to God. Certainly not to have God inside of him, but to have spoken to God and, therefore, there is no one who will ever achieve the gift that Moses has achieved.

Well, my goodness, what a curse on mankind!
To say that Moses could speak to God and no
one else could.
To say that indeed it was only Moses' ability to
speak to God—not truly to commune
with Him, and be one with Him.

Oh—yes, but that was the philosophy was it not?

Is that not what your Sunday school teachers have taught you, and what your adults have taught you—that you have no authority, that your teachings comes to you by way of others, by those who are said to be great Masters, priests, rabbis, monks, and whatnot. They are your spiritual leaders, and they tell you what God provides, and what He does not provide, and you have no opportunity whatsoever for having direct communion with God. Nonsense, my friends!

As we know, as you have learned from our teachings, each and every one of you have an opportunity to speak with God. [And] that is what Jesus taught to his disciples, and to those that were around him. You must also remember that Jesus, as a Master, is like every other Master—they give teachings according to the ability, [or] limited abilities of their disciples or students to learn. They give them a sequential teaching. Everyone who has ever been initiated into a path of mystery understands that there are certain limitations that they naturally face in the beginning and, therefore, that the teachings must be given in some sort of sequence or order—so be it. Jesus was no different, and the teachings that he gave to his direct disciples, the twelve, were far different than those that were given to the common people. Simply because he couldn't give an advanced teaching on the Sermon on the Mount to all the thousands assembled there without some preparation beforehand.

Now, what you must also understand is that many of

those individuals who came to the Sermon on the Mount, for instance, continued to stay with Jesus, and he had large assemblies, large groups of individuals, here and there scattered all over the countryside who he would go and visit from time to time and give new instructions. In addition to the twelve [disciples], there were many thousands that he spoke to personally, on a monthly basis, travelling around the countryside as you know he did, to teach to them, and to initiate them. To enter them into cleansing processes, both of diet—spiritually and emotionally—so that their bodies might be made clear, their spirit might be made clear, and their emotional form might be made clear to receive the light of God—yes.

And he would also teach them mantras, the words of God, the holy spoken words, the pronunciation of the *Yud heh vov heh*, and other associations with the divine name of God. Which it is said, according to the Hebrew tradition, that whosoever knows how to pronounce those syllables correctly would instantaneously know God. There is even a tradition in your now modern Jewish philosophy of the Haseidics of one who is named *Bal Shem Tov*, in other words, knower of the good word. He had a vision—yes, some time ago, in eastern Europe, about how to pronounce that divine name. All right . . . Well—we are not here to speak about those things, we are here to speak about Saint John.

At the end of Saint John's days, he went to a place called Ephesus. Ephesus is a recognized place of origin of wisdom. It was originally, in the ancient world, the place of the temple of Diana, goddess of wisdom. That temple was destroyed through various forms of black magic and interference in about the sixth or seventh century, B.C., by your counting. In truth, it was destroyed much earlier than that. There was an original temple of Diana before that one, that was part of the Atlantean world. A remnant of a much more ancient civilization that began about a million-and-a-half years ago to reconstruct temples that had been destroyed in the still earlier time period of Lemuria.

As you can see from this discussion, there were certain locations on the Earth where temples once existed and do not exist anymore. These temples were often reconstructed over time. The temple of Diana, the location of Ephesus, was part of a great sequence of wisdom. A vortex of wisdom exists there. A tremendous accelerating force emits out of the ground, or at least at one time emitted out of the ground. It has been slowed down as though the fissure has been closed.

But at that time [the end of Saint John's days], Saint John entered into his tomb, perfectly alive. He told no one to enter in after him. And he told them to seal up the tomb. Later, when it was examined, there was no body to be found. Again, [certain] ones thought, "OK, what happened?" A mystery.

Saint John ascended, just as Jesus ascended. He transmuted the physical cells of his body into light, therefore forming a physical form of light that could travel at will through the Heavens, enter up into the clouds and be whisked away into those realms that we call our worlds of other dimensions—you call them Heavens.

I must also clarify here that there are two Heavens—those of Earth, and those of Heaven. What do I mean by that? There are seven astral worlds that surround your planet Earth. They are commonly referred to as your *Earthly Heavens*. They are places of transformation and the housing of souls that are waiting to become, once again, third dimensional physical beings. This Heaven is a third dimensional Heaven. There are, as you may now suspect, many dimensions. Each dimension has its planets and its Heavens. It's physical worlds by that dimensional standard, and its non-physical worlds by that dimensional standard. We then say that anything beyond the third dimension is in a realm of Heaven, beyond the Earth and parallel to the Earth velocity—all right.

Saint John ascended beyond the seven astral worlds and went directly into Heaven. Before he did this, however, he was shown the steps, or stages, that he would go through. You see—Saint John was a scholar. He had a lot of knowledge behind him. He had studied intensely with Jesus and desired a great amount of authority and knowledge from Jesus. So he was given it. But the mystery that was never explained to him in enough detail was the process of Ascension, [of] which Jesus underwent—all right.

He had to have that experience, he desired it intensely, and he spent many, many hours when he was not teaching to the masses, studying his own enlightenment and the sequence and change of his internal being. This vision came to him. It truly was a *divine revelation.* Divine revelation means the light becomes so bright inside of oneself, filling ones heart with bliss and love that [it] overwhelms one, ecstasy occurs, and one nearly goes into a swoon it is so revitalizing!

Saint John had such an experience, and began to describe it. The first thing that he noticed in his description was the alpha and the omega, the beginning and end, for they are indeed the same. What he saw was that in the beginning it was all pure, and in the end it was all pure, and what happened in between was a sequence of history. A sequence of history—history unfolding by itself. He, therefore, also recognized that the alpha and omega would be surrounded by seven regions, seven candles. These seven candles are lights representing the different planetary regions, or regions of sequences of knowledge.

We can understand Saint John, by understanding that he was for all of his knowledge a simple man. And he recognized these things symbolically. The alpha and the omega was a bright light, a powerful force, a being of such tremendous strength and mighty power, and he saw indeed the flaming sword coming from its mouth. Well—this was an analogy you must understand. But in truth, there is *some truth* behind it.

As you may recall some of my discussions about the sword of Lord Michael—represents truth. It is the sword of truth [the flaming sword] that was given to all the twenty-four Elohim. The twenty-four elders were visualized by Saint John as surrounding the throne of God. Out of the throne came the sword. For the sword of truth came directly out of God. It was a two-edged sword. That meant it could be used both to create or destroy. What does that mean—to destroy? For from the perspective of God there is no such thing as destruction. There is change, however. The flaming sword, the sword of truth, wasn't a metallic sword at all, but it was a sword of [or representing] change—transformation. It consumes those things that are not useful—burns them up—creating something that is useful.

Saint John also understood this to be a part of what we could say is the *lineage*, or tradition of knowledge, the spoken word—coming from the mouth. How it is that as one becomes enlightened, or filled with light, that the desire for one to speak forth what one knows is so intense that one must speak it forth. And in truth, as Saint John was seeing the alpha and omega—he was getting a vision of his higher nature. And he was understanding that, that higher nature would not be completed upon the Earth until he spoke what he knew—until he wrote it down and translated it for the good of common man. Those masses that he taught to in the present, and that he would continue teaching to in the future, through his writings. All right . . .

He then spoke of the seven churches of Asia. There

is that number seven again! Let me explain right off that Earth is a vibration of seven tones, and seven colors. If you break up the light of God as it comes in, the light of [the] sun as it comes in to this dimension of the solar system, meaning your Earth, it is broken up into seven colors of the rainbow. You also will notice that throughout your Earth there are basically seven tones, although some of the Asiatic cultures, and other cultures of the Earth, have divided it up still further. It is based upon seven primary color sequences.

Seven tones,
Seven colors,
Seven frequencies,
Seven rays of light,
Seven dimensions within the third dimension.
Seven chakras in the human body.
Seven levels to the astral Heavens—seven.

The seven churches of Asia represented to Saint John the transition that he must undergo once he had realized the truth about God. Once he realized that all was the same in the beginning, as it is in the end, and he then realized the eternity of God. He realized that the expression of God's love and force into the universe was without precedent, and that it was contained within him. He then realized that his spiritual nature had to be transformed along with his physical nature. The sword emanating from the alpha and the omega represented to him not only the speaking forth of knowledge, but the reaching out of the divine Godhead into the Earth. Once it reached into the Earth it had to have its churches, its places of teaching, its temples of learning and transition. The seven churches of Asia are none other than the seven levels of Ascension, the seven rungs of the ladder of the Mithrac, the seven chakras of the body, the seven dimensional areas.

The first chakra being the chakra of Earth. The security of the Earth vibration, knowing that Earth will protect you. In the Ascension mode it is the last to move. It means that the very physical substance of the Earth must be completely absorbed into Heaven. We will see in the *Book of Revelations* two stages—[the first] climbing from the Earth, the second being the celestial Heaven of the crown chakra, the *brahmarandra* of the Hindus, the Crystal Heaven of the ancients. The Imperian Heaven of the Greeks.

The seventh chakra, the crown of the head, represents the highest and most unified of all knowledge. First, we would step up to that, then we bring it back to Earth—as we shall see. For after Saint John experiences the climbing of the seven ladders, the seven churches being visited, then he starts to find all manner of teachings beginning with the seven seals—right, yes. And the seven plagues that follow. And the beast of the number six, 666.

I must remind you that we are functioning in a world of seven, and if the seven is not complete, meaning the Godhead, you have a world of incomplete nature, six. [The] 666 is three dimensions—physical, mental, and spiritual. If six reigns, in not only the physical or the mental range but also the spiritual, [then] you have a beast on your hands that is out of control. Seven must be complete before Earth is complete. Then comes the transition, or transmutation, of the physical system of the Earth. All right . . .

The first church to be visited was Ephesus. Ephesus, where Saint John ascended. Ephesus represented his step from the Earth into the first Heaven, because Ephesus is also recognized to be the temple of Diana of the ancients—it also represents the moon. Of course, if you are stepping off the Earth into Heaven, you are going to first step on the moon. The moon is your reflective nature. It is what could be recognized as watery, for the moon influences the waters. By way of the chakras then we would understand.

The first chakra to be that of Earth.

The second chakra to be that of water or the
            moon—relationships.
Relationships between all human Beings.

We are finding that as you complete of your Earthly life, you must be in harmony with the Earth before you can leave it. You must feel at peace with it. You must feel peace with your relationships as well.

Next—you must understand your Soul nature,
            that is the third chakra, the solar plexus.

Here is also the world of fear, and of course, fear will come up as you are ascending. It is part of the transition. It is part of the functioning of life itself in a world that is incomplete and not full of knowledge. Fear is the result of the unknown. Fear only becomes released when you know the nature of your Soul to be one with God.

The third chakra then, the third rung on the ladder that is, is the recognition that one must be in balance with oneself before one can ascend any farther. One must know the limitations of fear, and the unlimited nature of the Soul, free of fear.

Next, one enters into the full integration then of Earth with Heaven—Heaven with Earth. This is the heart center, the center of love and balance. Balance truly must occur as you are ascending. Not only between Earth and spirituality, but between your male and female natures as well. That which desires out of will, and that which desires out of reception, passivity—to receive, to be nurtured, to be taken care of.

One recognizes on the path of Ascension then,
as one climbs the ladder of the heart [the fourth chakra] that truly life is a balance between God and man.
Between the cooperative efforts of God and man.

Mankind is a vehicle to receive God's love, and then

it is God's power. It is like the fuel, the gasoline, of the human condition. The human spirit is fueled by God, and motivated to move ahead. Yes—male and female, acceptance and action. Reception and activity—male and female. All right . . .

Next, once one receives the fuel of God, and it is balanced and harmonized, Heaven with Earth—everything of Earth is balanced in Heaven and accepted by Heaven, everything of Heaven is balanced by Earth and accepted by Earth, male and female are both balanced, none stepping on each other—then we begin to express God's truth, and that is the throat chakra.

> [The throat chakra, the fifth chakra, is] the fifth
> rung of the ladder.

And out of that, as we begin to express God's truth, come all of the miracles. The miracles must unfold, as we would climb the ladder of Ascension. Saint John was known to have performed miracles, as were most of the disciples. As they were on that path of Ascension they needed to express their Godliness, their ability of the God within them to perform that which is beyond all limitation and the miraculous.

> The sixth chakra was that of insight, the third
> eye as you would call it, the visionary.

Indeed the very function of the vision of Apocalypse

has to do with that insight and revelation. Seeing the mystery and understanding the mystery. The things that could not be understood simply by walking on Earth. No mortal mind can read the *Book of Revelations* and understand it without someone to interpret it for them. Until that time arises, when they originate the vision within their own third eye, within the vehicle of insight, within their physical form, then, my friends, the *Book of Revelations* will truly be *revelationary* to you.

The final rung of the ladder, the seventh, is the completion—the crown chakra.

The crown chakra is represented by the Hindus as a thousand petalled lotus. By the ancients as a crystal, the crystal cave you might say. A crystal has many facets, doesn't it? And it is absolutely clear. The thousand-petalled lotus of the Asiatics just simply represents that this is the control center. It is that which unifies and harmonizes all the functions of life.

The brain, which is the physical substance reflective of the crown chakra, has a lot to do with the thousand petalled lotus. For, as your scientists have discovered, along the brains surface there is a response point [for] every portion of the body, every organ, every limb. The thousand petalled lotus must be harmonized and unified with the one. All the functions of life must be harmonized with the one, and then one is said to be *enlightened*. The seven churches had to be cleared and cleansed. Beginning with Ephesus, all the way up to the final. So be it . . .

In the ancient world of astronomy, by the way, the seventh also had much to do with the planet Saturn. Saturn, for those of you who don't know, is the seat of the brotherhoods and sisterhoods of light. It is the world, or solar government, for this solar system. Astrologically speaking, to your astrologers Saturn represents the planet of karma. It represents the planet of karma because it is the overseership, [that is where] karma is to be completed. The beings that have completed their karma reside on Saturn, and it is their hope that all beings complete their karma and become liberated and one with God. So Saturn's influence then will be to complete karma, and not put it off for another day. The final rung of the ladder must, therefore, include the planet Saturn—astrologically speaking—for it must be the planet that liberates one from karma. All right . . .

Next, is the complete vision of that which is called the *throne of God*. And in the throne of God one sees that there is a Being, holding a tiny book—a book that is said to carry the seven seals—and that no one on Earth or in Heaven is seen as worthy of opening the book. This is where we get a very clear explanation of the third dimension. For here we are describing not only the physical condition of Earth, but its Heavenly condition as well.

If you were to look at your astral worlds, you know this by speaking to certain spirit guides [you would know] that they are ready for their incarnation to a new form. That these Beings have not yet completed their Earthly karma and, therefore, still are prone to bias, prejudice, and error. And though they have great insight from the other side, from your perspective, they are yet locked into the third dimensional thinking as you are. That is why none of Heaven and Earth are worthy of opening the book. For in order to open the book, that carries the seals of God, one must be *enlightened*.

The seals of God—what does this mean? What are the seven seals of the book—what is the book? The *book* is simply the book of wisdom. It is the *Book of Life*—eternal life. When one opens eternal life, in a physical condition, one instantly gains the recognition of God. Well—what does this mean?

The recognition of God is an infinite vision. If it were to come into a lamp, the lamp would shatter. This is the vision of the Zohar, by the way, when the lamps are filled with the presence of God, they shattered. Right in the very beginning of the Zohar it talks about that—in its discussion on Genesis. *Breshith* is the Hebrew word. So you see, my friends, that this vision couldn't be opened by anyone. What would happen? What did happen as the seven seals were opened?

The seven seals represent God's love and light pouring into the Earth, that is still unprepared, [and] has not prepared itself for completion. The vision then that follows for Saint John, is a vision that everyone will go through to some degree. But how much of a degree is yet the question.

It might be indeed fearful and full of confusion. The bad will get more wicked, and the righteous will get more righteous, it is said. But, my friends, I want you to know something. "None of the bad needs to get worse!" These are the souls that are resisting their evolution. They are turning their backs upon God—meaning God is the ability to *see*.

They are turning their backs upon what they are seeing, and pretending that it just doesn't exist. Well—I believe that describes most of your leaders, doesn't it. It describes most of you here, from situation to situation. That situation must be relieved, it must be transformed. And as the light of God comes pouring in, it will be transformed. Because light will only get brighter. That means the things from which you are turning away from, that you do not want to look at, that are perhaps too painful to visualize, to face, for one reason or another. I say to you, my friends, "You will face them!" You will change them and transform them, or you will be turned into another dimension where the fire and brimstone exists, which is simply the perpetuation of the world just as you have known it. You will continue to exist under a circumstance of karma, not here on Earth, but prepared for you elsewhere.

God's love is so gracious, that even if you choose to continue to destroy yourself through cycles of birth and death, through pain and suffering—you may so choose. God's love is that great for you!

He would, of course, prefer that you choose everlasting life and joyous harmony with all of good existence, including coming back to His inheritance. But if you choose to ignore your inheritance and go off on your own, as the prodigal Son or Daughter, then—so be it. You may do so, it is your choice.

But there is a warning here, and that is the warning of the seven seals. By the way—the throne of God was surrounded by seven lamps. These were the seven spirits of God. The seven lamps represent the light—the light coming in to the seven dimensions, the seven chakras. Awakening within you the seven ways of looking at the world that I described earlier. The particular ones to be of notice at this time are the first three.

The first chakra, which is Earth;
The second chakra which is water or rela-
        tionships, and;
The third chakra which is fire or individuality,
        or ego—the Power Center.

Most of you are healing in your heart, and balancing your male and female Heaven on Earth. You are starting to recognize that on the spiritual path. Most of you are also— as much as you are jammed up in the throat and are afraid to say what you are thinking and feeling—communicating what you want. You are doing it—you are getting better at it. I would say that your expression factors have more to do with the first three chakras than with the fourth, fifth, and sixth.

So—your first three issues will be beginning with the third chakra, getting in alignment with your own beliefs and truth—finding yourself. No longer fearing who you are and having to compromise it. Releasing yourself from fear. Only when you know who you are can you enter into a relationship with others. Then you will find that you must respect their needs as well as your own. That is true relationship. You will no longer force them to change, no longer forcing yourself to change. You will have mutual loving allowance in the second chakra clearing. The first chakra being finally to be in balance and harmony with everything on Earth. Meaning that you look to the Earth and it will support you. It will love you and nurture you. I shall repeat that again.

Most of the clearing that is taking place on Earth at this time has to do with: One, the clearing of the third chakra—which is getting in touch and loving self. That means trusting yourself. Taking care of yourself and trusting who you are. No longer compromising out of fear. The second chakra, which is the next one to be cleared, means trusting yourself with others. That means knowing that others will approve of you and that you can approve of them. That means that you will live in [a] loving relationship with them, both collectively, personally, intimately, and sexually—all of those. Being in relationship with others, in a personal manner, and still being able to be yourself, and be with them as they are themselves. Quite a balancing act, I must say, but it shall take place, and it is taking place even at this time.

The final, is your relationship with the Earth. As you are in relationship to yourself and with others you must also look at the Earth and say, "She approves of me." What I do I will be supported for, and the Earth will not only support me but love my actions and know that I am benefiting the Earth—that I am not only of mutual benefit to my loved ones, and my friends, but to all of the Earth. When that is finally healed you are ready, my friends, for Heaven. The gates of Heaven will be opened unto you, and indeed that is precisely what happened with Saint John, as we shall shortly see.

Now—along comes the lamb... What was the lamb? In the ancient world, it was the lamb that was sacrificed. And this was a lamb that had already been slain. The lamb was filled with light. It is commonly associated with Jesus—yes, the lamb. The lamb is also the lion of Juda. I believe the lion was one of the beasts that stood in front of the throne, wasn't it? Along with the bull. Along with the eagle, and man. These represented the four primary religions of the Earth. The four primary views. The lion being the Jewish religion, the Hebrew religions, including the Christian religion at that time. The bull being that of the other cultures of the middle east, into the Hindus, for the Hindus often worshipped the bull, did they not? The eagle being that of those which were of the Americas, north and south. And man—that was the culture farther east into certain areas of Asia, no longer in existence by the way—which understood mankind to be its own savior. Well—there were certain philosophies throughout the world at that time [such as] the Greeks for instance, where they believed that mankind would be its own savior. These were the four religions standing before the throne of God. Each with their own view and perspective.

When the lamb came along it represented the sacrifice of all of them, for lambs were sacrificed by all religions at that time. It represented the Ascension, one who had already merged with God, sacrificing their Earthly karma, transmuting themselves on behalf of others. Why do you sacrifice a lamb? Well—for abundance of course. There's no other reason. You give what you have in order to receive more. You give it to God to receive more. The sacrifice of the lamb has to do with that request for abundance.

The lamb's vision then was a natural one in that time period, and Jesus was the shining star! He came to Saint John and showed to him that he was the one capable of opening the book. He had indeed died for the sins of the Earth. To clear up the misconceptions and allusions that had perpetuated themselves since the time and fall of Atlantis. And it was now time for the ascended form of Jesus to come along and to open the book and to talk about all of that which was to be known—the mysteries, the four beasts, the four major religions then would bow down before that one. This does not necessarily mean that all the religions of the Earth will bow down to Christianity. For indeed the Christians are as much at fault in their knowledge of God as everyone else. It simply means that—that which is the religion or dogmatic teachings of the Earth will see one throne. They will all have their names or descriptions of it, but it will be the same throne. And they will have to have that one, the shining one, who has walked upon the Earth, understood the Earth, to reveal it to them. Who is that one? Why, my friends, it is none other than yourself!

The throne of God that you are witnessing is within you, the religion surrounds it, it is your understanding of that throne. And therefore, when your Christ consciousness comes to you and awakens and reveals itself to you and you take your seat upon the throne, your religion will bow down to that Christ authority in you. In other words—as I was saying before—suddenly, you will read the *Book of Revelations* and understand it. You will understand things in your religion that you have never understood before. You will understand them firsthand. That is the true meaning of this—that is why the book can be opened by you. For your inner Christ consciousness can reveal all of those things to you.

Well—let us look at the seven seals. The first four have to do with the horsemen of the Apocalypse. Many are talking about the horsemen coming. I already mentioned about the one on the white horse, both in this book and in the book of the Hindus. The Kalki coming on a white horse, also carrying a sword, I might add.

In this case, the one on the white horse was wearing a crown and holding a bow.

The next comes on a red horse, carrying a great
     sword.
Then a black horse, holding a pair of balances.
And, finally, it's death coming on a pale horse—
     and all of hell follows him!

Well—what does this mean? These are the transitions of life, my friend. The horse represents something moving through time. These are the transitions through time. Whether we speak of them as the Hindus [do], as four Yuga's—four ages of time, or whether we speak of them as the four ages of life—your birth, followed by childhood or youth, maturity, then death—those being the four periods of life. Or whether we look at it as the present day—the final four years, each bringing a different truth.

There are those in the first wave, we will call them waves now rather than horses, the first wave being a wave of white light or illumination. That occurred already, my friends, with that which is called the Harmonic Convergence—it was the first horse, and [in Saint John's vision] that horse was to continue for some time. It is said in the Hindus tradition that Kalki rides around the Earth gathering up the enlightened Souls. This is the same tradition. The white horse will gather up, lift up through illumination, many individuals on Earth whose job it is to help to assist others with their awakening process.

Those that do not ride the first wave, will have an opportunity again. Although the second wave is a little more difficult. Why? Because they are more stubborn individuals. They didn't want to ride [the white horse], the first wave, and so they are going to have to ride the second one. And so—here comes the red horse, carrying a great sword. What is the great sword? The great sword is that which is cutting through all of the nonsense. It is a sword of truth of Lord Michael.

Lord Michael, in this past March and April of 1990, said that he had returned to slay the dragon—that the prophesy has now begun. And [in] this time period he is moving over the Earth with his great and mighty sword. Releasing the old mold of karma. And this is on a red horse, a red horse, for emotions. The emotions are being stirred up and every soul on Earth, no matter how powerful or how insignificant, you are all experiencing at this time the red horse. The transformation of emotional energy into spiritual light. Do not resist it, my friends. It is your horse to Heaven! Ride this horse—let it take you where you must go. And indeed I say to you, "You will end up in Heaven, and ascended." Saint John had to do it. Lord Jesus had to do it. Every great saint on Earth had to go through their emotional trials.

The trial of Jesus on the desert had much to do with the emotional, dogmatic confusion that took place inside of him. One force saying *this*, another force saying *that*, his parents and society saying *come and have your riches, come and do this, come and do that. . .this will give you joy, this will give you happiness*. But Jesus understood—as he was there in the desert—that he was all alone with God. And that there was nothing else that he needed. That's why he was on a desert! There was nothing else that he needed but God—all right. The next horse. If you miss this [horse], it gets worse—oh, yes! You think that your emotions are difficult? They're only going to get worse.

The next horse, is a black horse. [It represents] all the drudgeries of your subconscious, all the gunk that's down in there. Well, what happens when you mix all the colors together, and you start to suppress all of your emotions—it is a black form. Anyone that can see the aura will tell you that there are certain places in everyone's aura where it is black. Black because the concentration of emotional energy, and pain, and suffering is so intense. The black horse [represents] all the things that you absolutely do not want to look at. Well, my friends, you are going to have to look at them!

When the black horse comes—and I believe the black horse is already starting to peek its head over the horizon, that is why you are given an opportunity to ride the red horse, you can clear it now, you do not have to wait for the black one—[for] when the black horse comes, the man who is riding it, or the woman, the Being of Light, is holding a pair of balances. This means the reason that it is coming is to create balance—not disharmony. It is here to create balance. You can ride the dark horse and it will take you to balance. It is the most fearful horse to ride, but nonetheless, it will take you to balance. If you miss that one, then you will wait for death.

Death is the last horse. Now—death means the end—but the end of what? If life is eternal—what is this death? It rides on a pale horse, and all hell follows it. If you put off till last—if you are one of the last ones to go through the healing process—I believe you are in for a hell of a time! I believe [it is] that which is all of the damnation that you have created for yourself, all of those things.

And what does this mean—to be damned?
It means to say, "I am not going to look at you (it)."
It means that it is so unuseful to me, so painful to me, so unwanted or unloved by me, that it has been *damned* by me.
And that means that it has been dammed up inside the personality and will finally come out in the end.
Death cures all.
Death is transition—it is the end of the old— it rides a pale horse.

For now it has the opportunity to complete. As we enter into that which is this final reality, one of two things is going to happen. You will feel like you are losing touch—can't grab a hold of that horse—that is why it is pale. Or, that you are becoming transparent—meaning moving into light. If you are losing touch it means that you are still not wishing to face things and you just want to go through the process of death again—forget about it all. Hopefully, to wake up the next day and [find] it will all be over and you can continue life as you have been.

These Souls, as I mentioned, will be given an opportunity to continue their life elsewhere, with karma. Somewhere other than Earth. But Earth, my friends, will not carry karma any more. Those of you who remain here will pass into the higher form which is the transparent form of light. There, you will release all of that which has been the hell inside of you. And you will release it once and for all. It will have died, never to return—you will have awakened, never to go asleep again.

You have faced all of your issues, and you have united them all with God in a higher understanding and harmony and peace within yourself. Those are the four horsemen. Each one coming on a wave that will sweep over humanity. Lifting them into their divine state. And this is what is happening in this next half a decade—all right.

Following the four horsemen, there was a great release that Saint John saw. [And he saw] all of the Souls that had been crucified, or slain because of their religious nature, being released for Ascension. Now—this meant these may be Souls that had not truly ascended themselves. They hadn't received their full illumination but they committed themselves to the path, even against that which was their society—and their society persecuted them for it. It is said that in that time—because of their commitment to God and to harmony, even though they didn't get full realization—once the four horsemen come, even if they have resisted, those Souls will be released and lifted up into Heaven as well. So if you are one of those Souls, don't worry my friends, you will be taken care of. But, best to ride the best horse—hmmm! Yes—choose a white one, not a pale one—all right—next!

When the sixth seal was opened, the Earth began to quake. Not only did the Earth quake, but the sun darkened, and the moon was filled with blood. The Earth quaking represents the physical body in transformation. All of your beliefs are stored in your bodies. As the Earth, your body, begins to receive the light of Heaven, it begins to shake. You will often find physical[ly] distressing ailments with your cleansing process, and with your healing process. The sun will become darkened, meaning—when those things happen to you, when the Earth quakes, when the things go wrong, the illumination or guidance of your spiritual nature will become darkened and you will forget. And you will complain, and you will say, "I am not worth a thing, [and] my moon", which is your own Soul or divine Soul, "has become bloodied—I am now in pain on Earth, everything is going wrong, where is God?"

Yes—my friends, you will say it, you will feel it, you will complain, and yet you can also pass through it. For, at that point the angels of the winds will come—and the angels of the winds are the angels of change—they will create change and transformation. Allow the process to continue, don't stop it. Don't hold the sun in a darkened state, or the moon in a bloodied state, or the Earthquakes constantly quaking. Don't try to hold back, do not resist those quakes, let the body cleanse, let the emotions cleanse, let your doubts come up and let them be answered. The angels of the winds are the winds of change, and they *will* heal and transform you.

Next—another angel comes to awaken the 144,000. This has two meanings, the microcosm, and the macrocosm. For the entire planet there are 144,000 Souls of Light. These Souls of Light volunteered with Sunat Kamara and Jesus, or Sananda, back at the time of Atlantis, and just before Atlantis in the later stages of Lemuria. These 144,000 souls are ascended Souls, they are Souls that are Masters of Light and Wisdom, who have come voluntarily to assist this Earth in its awakening, and have been with Earth for as long as time remembered. They are still here working in various capacities. Many of them with a sort of veil over them. They will be awakened. At that point, 144,000 Souls will start to move around the Earth to save as many other Souls as they can. To awaken those Souls, to bring them Light, and Power, and Love.

It is said that [in the body] there are 144,000 receptors of light. According to the Hindus there are 72,000 nadi's in the human body, 72,000 nervous endings. But they forgot that there is a male and female. If you would take male and female, each having 72,000, I believe the sum of the two is 144,000. So—once again we see the relationship between the east and the west coinciding. [These] 144,000 light endings in the human body are the nerve endings, your visionary endings, your perception endings, that must become illumined with the spirit of God. Meaning—all of your nervous system, all of your abilities to perceive, must be filled with a vision of God. Then all the cells around them, collectively, will start to magically transform. When you have 144,000 nerve endings in your body fully illuminated, your whole body will begin to transform.

When the Earth quakes, these coverings, [which are] just like a covering of mud over a light bulb, will be broken. The mud will no longer hide the light, and the light will shine and every cell will be filled with it. The seventh seal, the last one, after the 144,000 were illuminated, starts off with a half an hour of silence. That peace that comes from the 144,000 awakening is quite profound. It is, "Aaahhh, at last, we are finally moving into peace." . . . all right.

But following that, there are seven angels coming. Each were given a trumpet, and the seven trumpets began to blow. I must remind you of the seven levels, the seven chakras. The angels come, and they blow their trumpets. I must also remind you that the seven levels are the seven dimensions of the Earth. The seven tones of the Earth, the seven colors of the rainbow, the seven tones of the trumpets will blare loudly, and they will literally cause a quickening in each of the chakras causing final transformation and awakening.

When the trumpets played the seven tones—catastrophes occurred, because those things that were not yet in purity, [and] had not yet been built out of the substance of God, would begin to shake and catastrophes would occur. Meaning—those things that you have done, that you hide from, that cause you problems over and over again, the things that come out of your mouth at the wrong moment—all of those things that you consider catastrophe, they are hidden and buried inside of you, and if you have not faced them at that moment, when the final tone comes, when the final light shines, they will be revealed to you. It doesn't mean in any of these cases that catastrophes are caused by the second coming of the Christ energy to the Earth. They were here beforehand, and now simply exposed.

Over and over again I must say to you, my friends, "That which is revelation is revealing those things which have been hidden." The catastrophes have been here, you have witnessed them again and again. The light is only shining on them. When the seven trumpets blare, the final elements that have been hidden must then still come out. One of which is the most difficult will occur. The two stars, one [of which is] called Wormwood, would fall from the Heaven, and another would fall, given the key to the bottomless pit from which all evil was issued. My friends, these two stars in Heaven represent the vision, the Earthly visions, the worldly visions, of religion. The Wormwood that has plagued your world since the beginning.

What is the Wormwood? I [have] spoke[n] to you [of] why the fall occurred. You tasted of the fruit of good and evil in the garden of Eden. Paradise was your alpha, paradise is your omega. When you taste, however, of the Wormwood, it will be bitter. When you taste of the fruit of good and evil, when you make things right and wrong, you are automatically creating your bitterness. You are creating the rights and wrongs. You have a choice to do that. You have every right to do it, if you would like to. But I must recommend to you not to. You have done it already. Your society has done it, and has placed it in the Heavens as part of your religion—that Wormwood will fall to the Earth. For some, it will fall into a bottomless pit. For indeed, where you blame yourself, it has no bottom. You will continue to do so endlessly. That is your choice—if you wish to fall into the bottomless pit of blame, of right and wrong. The stars will fall from the Heaven, and when they do fall from the Heaven what is remaining in Heaven is pure.

Then an angel came and offered to John a little book to eat. A little book—of wisdom—hmmm. And he ate it, and he was fully illumined, and he ascended.

In the next several chapters of the *Book of Revelations* there are many images, and I would like to just touch upon them briefly. One is a woman clothed with the sun, who had the moon under her feet and a crown of twelve stars. Well—and out of that came a war in Heaven— Armageddon.

Armageddon began to occur. Although that is more completely mentioned later on, in truth it began when the woman was clothed with the sun. This is the feminine age that is dawning. It is not an age of trying to make things happen. It is an age in which you will tune in to what God desires in you to happen, which [in] your higher nature happens. You will no longer be forcing the people around you to change. You will no longer be damning yourselves for the things that you could not do. You will be like a woman—receiving of God's love. Clothed in the sun—meaning clothed in the golden light of God. You will stand on the moon, the moon meaning your human personality. This means that you will rely on your human personality to yet conduct affairs of Earth, but it will be blended with the sun.

> The sun and moon will be one.
> It will be feminine in nature.
> Not aggressive—but passive, benevolent, nurturing.
> And you will be surrounded by a crown of twelve stars—not seven.
> The natural vibration of God is twelve.
> There are twelve frequencies of the highest Heavens—not seven.

I [have] said [before] that beyond the seven astral worlds there are additional vibrations and dimensions.

> In all, there are twelve frequencies of light,
> Twelve tones,
> Twelve stars,

Twelve chakras—in other words.
Twelve visionary dimensions and realizations.

You will be crowned with all twelve when you move
into Ascension. And the beast of the 666 vibration will come
out of the sea with his seven heads, and his ten horns—
hmmm. The ten horns are the five organs of action, and the
five organs of perceptions—yes. That is the way that the
worldly beast expresses himself. He has seven heads
because he looks through seven different perspectives of the
chakras, the seven different dimensions of the astral world.
But yet he is a beast.

He is worldly by nature, he is of the vibration of 666.
That means actually he is incomplete and his mental,
physical, emotional, or spiritual worlds, 666, [are] incomplete—not 777. The 666 must move to 777, and finally into
the 888 of Jesus. Jesus is said to have the vibration of 888.
If you turn an eight on its side, it is infinite. That means,
infinity in the physical, infinity in the mental, infinity in the
emotional and spiritual planes. We are evolving from 666
to balance the 777, and move into the 888 of the true divinity
of spirituality. Yes, the eighth chakra will start to open. The
eighth vibration, the dimensions beyond the seven will
begin to be illuminated and will be pure white light, and pure
harmony and peace. Yes—all right.

Next—we see the lamb on Mount Zion, with the
144,000. An angel announces the fall of Babylon. When
you have all ascended to the top of the mountain you will

recognize that Babylon, or your worldliness, is falling away. That does not mean that you will not have a world, that you will not be doing things the way that you had. That you will not have your houses, and your vocations, and your families—indeed you will. But they will not mean what they mean to you today.

> They will all be seen in the light of God.
> You will see God shining in every loved one.
> You will see God in every house.
> You will see a reason for every person on Earth.
> You will no longer fear them getting ahead of you, for you will recognize it is all in divine harmony, and for the greater good of society.
> You will recognize that every cell in God's body has a place of importance.

The angel announcing the fall of Babylon is just that shining state of Heaven in every cell. Then it is said that one like a shining one, like the son of man, comes with a sickle for the harvest, riding a cloud. And he reaps the ripened grain. That means that basically the shining light, which is your higher self, will come and lift you. Your ripened grains mean that you are ready for bursting forth with your spiritual dimension. The shining one, the son of man, will come and harvest you. Your higher self will harvest you.

Otherwise, another angel comes. This is the one who

is called the angel of death. With a sickle to capture the ripened vines of the Earth. The vines of the Earth that are thrown into the winery or the wine press of the wrath of God. What does the wrath of God mean? Well—it doesn't mean that God is going to come and punish them all. It means that they have already punished themselves. That they are yet resisting. They are trying to compress their existence, rather than expand it, and they are finding themselves being pressured into these situations of pain, and it will indeed feel like the wrath of God to them. My friends, hopefully, at that point the angel of death will not need to come with a sickle. For all of humanity will have ascended and [have] been reaped by the angel of light—So be it.

If that doesn't happen, however, there will be seven plagues. The seven plagues are the final purging of the chakras. We've seemingly gone through this over and over again, haven't we? The cleansing of the body—the final battle. Because after the seven plagues come, and the purging and cleansing of the chakras, once again we have the white horse and rider. And the rider at this time is called faithful and true—and Armageddon begins. The final war of light and darkness.

But this means that there are many opportunities until this point comes. In about five or six years, you will be experiencing this on this Earth. You will find, that approximately 1995 to 1997, there will be a war of light and darkness. There will be the forces of good and evil battling each other within each and every individual on Earth. There will be total chaos, *if* all has not transformed by that time.

You will, as I have said, be given many opportunities for transformation. How does one transform? Receive the light—trust. What is the rider of the white horse? He is faithful and true. This means the one that is to survive the transition is the one that rides the white horse of illumination, is faithful and true. Meaning—he or she *trusts*. That all of the transformations that are occurring are for the good, [are] for the better, not for the worse. That they are rising above them to the top of Mount Zion to join with the lion and the lamb and the 144,000. To indeed trust that all the transitions and waves that have come to completely throw mankind into a chaos are for a good reason. To bless mankind, and to bring them into a more awakened state. The war between light and darkness will end instantly when the faithful and true within you begins to have faith and trust. And recognize that the truth is the cleansing will occur, and it will be finalized and finished. Darkness will be replaced by light, and evil will be vanquished forever—into the lake of fire and brimstone—the evil, meaning that it will be removed from this Earth.

Those Souls that wish to continue with karma, and with pain and emotional distress, will be given an opportunity elsewhere to have it. That is all. It is quite simple. The *Judgement Book* will then be open. And all of those names who are not in there will be given an opportunity to go to the next world. In other words, the *Judgement Book* isn't *a* judgement book, it's just a book of all those individuals who have chosen to remain with the new Earth.

Then the new Earth and the new Heaven awaken!

It doesn't say in the *Book of Revelations* that everything was destroyed. It says that a new Earth and new Heaven will be created. And the new Jerusalem *shall come like a bride to a bridegroom, descending out of Heaven.* The new Jerusalem represents the new city, the new order of life, the new society, the new illumined state. The new Jerusalem is also the city of lights in the body. The 144,000 nadi's of the body are fully awakened—the full enlightenment. Not only the personal individual, but of the entire world. The twelve gates will be opened with transparent golden streets.

My goodness, what a wonderful image!
The twelve gates.
The twelve chakras—not just the seven.
The twelve illumined states.
The twelve vibrations of God.
All twelve vibrations moving together equals
golden Light, therefore golden streets.
Seven colors merged together equals white
Light.
Twelve colors merged together—the twelve
primary colors, seven of Earth, five
more of Heaven— when the twelve
colors have merged together it forms
the golden Light, or the halo.
The golden street of God.

So that your path is always filled with God, no
matter where you go.

This my friends, is the vision of the Apocalypse—the
Armageddon. Well—yes, you will be experiencing it. You
will have your crucifixions and your transformations. Your
body will become sick at times, or filled with pain. Your
emotions will become insurmountable. The sun will be
blotted out, and the moon filled with blood—some times.

But, my friends, have faith, ride the white horse.
Know that it is all in the destiny and path of spirituality that
you are cleansing. What I didn't mention to you [beforehand],
about those different groups that Jesus taught, [is that] the
different individuals that he would come visit once a month
[were] given their fastings to cleanse the body. He would
give them their emotional sequences to purge the soul of its
emotional distress. And indeed when they would go through
a cleansing, all sorts and manners of ailments would be
eliminated from the body. The fasting and the cleansing will
be necessary. You will have to purge many false elements
from your own bodies. They are not healthy. They all have
some sort of distress within them which can be cured.

My friends, all of this is in the path of beauty, in the
path of cleansing. All of the elements that you see going
wrong on the Earth will be righted. The Earth changes will
not occur—we will not let them. California will not fall into
the sea. The map [of the Earth changes] that is now
spreading around the United States, and around the world I

notice, showing large portions of the major metropolis areas all being under water, etc., is only an *analogy*. The water represents the cleansing of emotion. There will be much more concentration of cleansing in the big cities than there will be in the countryside. That is because the cities have greater power. We will see them transform more vigorously then elsewhere.

I would say, if I were one living on Earth, that I would choose to go through a vigorous change in order to get it over with and have a great power resulting from me. I would not hide out in the mountains somewhere waiting for it to be over. Because by hiding out, you may be one that is having to face the final horseman.

You know, my friends, where you hide, the light will find you. And what you are hiding from—all the evil—you must see. For it is only then that you will change it. The evil that you see is in you. It is your judgements of right and wrong—it is your painful beliefs. It is the ways in which you look on another and feel pain even without asking them whether they do in truth dislike you. My friends, you have many elements inside. In other speakings I have gone into each of these.

I encourage you to take the path of Light.
To ride the white horse—the wave of white
    Light.
The harmonizing of the seven chakras.
The seven dimensions, the seven colors, the

seven tones.

My friends, the Earth changes will not be that severe. There will not be large loss of life. It is our prediction at the current time that a full ninety percent of all humanity will make it through the transition. We are yet working to save the other ten percent. Hopefully, in the next five years that too will be accomplished. Help us, in whatever way you can, by spreading the message that this is not all doom and gloom. That this is merely a transition into a greater realization.

> Your Earth changes, well—they are there so
> that you recognize and value your
> Mother Earth.
> Taking care of her before you destroy her.
> Do not tear down her forests, and her lands for
> your cities.
> Do not pollute her waters and her air.
> Honor her—love her!
> For by polluting her you are killing yourselves.
> It is the destruction of yourself that you are
> perpetuating.

The Light is only going to show you what you are doing wrong. When you are in the dark and cannot see anything, then you know no better. But once the Light shines, you know. It is then your choice to choose. The Light will continue shining until you have backed into a corner. Then you will have to choose.

Blessings to you! All is Light, and Light is prevailing, and it is faithful and true. My dearest friends, I welcome you into the New Age. A New Age of new Heaven and a new Earth.

My blessings to you, and all of the Masters blessings with me. **Blessings to you . . . blessings . . . blessings . . . blessings . . .**

OM SELAH!

OTHER MATERIALS FOR PHYSICAL AND SPIRITUAL AWAKENING

A Mighty Feast For The Soul

COMING IN 1992 . . .

YOUR GUIDEBOOK TO ASCENSION HEALING

A Guidebook to Creating Your Ascension
and Uniting The Body with its Highest Goals
By Dr. Linda A. Fickes

This text provides a thorough understanding of ascension anatomy, healing principles and techniques for the professional healer, and the healer in you. Learn how to be in charge of your own healing process, how to use intuition with discrimination, how to listen to the body, and how to take assistance from our many helpers, the angels and Ascended Masters.

. . . COMING IN 1992

THE BEST OF MERLIN:
The Mystical, Magical, Master Merlin from Camelot

from Master Merlin
As Channeled by Bob Fickes

A Fascinating Text of Powerful Discourses on Dreams, Sex, Death, Self-Esteem, Chakras, Health and Well Being, UFO's, and much, much more!

OTHER AUDIO CASSETTES
AVAILABLE FROM
The Council of Light, Inc.
RELATED TO INFORMATION
CONTAINED IN THIS TEXT
AS CHANNELED BY BOB FICKES:

Michael Slays the Dragon
from Lord Michael
Events Leading to the Crucifixion and Resurrection
from Lord Jesus
Initiation of Ascension
from Master Serapis Bey
Address to High Council
from Saint Germaine
A New Orbit Around the Milky Way
from Lord Lanto and Saint Germaine
Ascension/Faith, Hope and Charity
from Lord Michael

The Council of Light, Inc.
CATALOGUE
A Catalogue of Materials for Ascension

A Mighty and Powerful Feast Awaits You,
Of Heart and Spirit,
An Abundant Banquet of High Quality Energy Material,
for Spiritual Awakening

For Additional Information Please Contact:

The Council of Light, Inc.
P. O. Box 670
Mount Shasta, California 96067
or
4400-4 Kalanianaole, #102
Honolulu, Hawaii 96821